MW00744399

The Carnie Kid tells all

Ilan Fisher

Edited by Pat Goudey

The Tamarac Press, Warren, Vermont
January, 2002

Published at
The Tamarac Press: Pat Goudey, publisher
291 Tamarac Street
Warren, Vermont 05674
pg@warrenslittle.com

Printed in USA
First Edition

Magic Ice

For Jody, Tamara, Zev and Big Mama;
and in memory of Big Daddy

Yes; as the music changes,
Like a prismatic glass,
It takes the light and ranges
Through all the moods that pass;
Dissects the common carnival
Of passions and regrets,
And gives the world a glimpse of all
The colours it forgets.

The Barrel-Organ
Alfred Noyes

Contents

Introduction vii
The first Thanksgiving ever (1992) 1
Duckies and bunnies (1990) 4
No free ride (1989) 8
Kindergarten chemistry (1994). 11
In the catbird seat (1990) 14
Marciano's magical mitts (1993) 16
Ellis: Island in the sun (1990) 19
Obituary: Blue Fish Special (1989) 22
The Carnie Kid rides again (1994) 23
Rolling with the punches (1992) 26
Stones: Earth Science *vs.* Biology (1994) 28
A short campaign (1994) 31
A town in two acts (1990) 33
Presidential poultry (1992) 36
Republicans head out (1990) 39
When sparks flew (1989) 41
Saints and saucers fly (1990) 43
New years, old stories (1992) 45
Soul music (1990) 47
New Guys (1994) 50
Tracks (1990) 52
The school that teaches from memory (1990). 55
Dead to rights (1992) 59
It never rains but it pours (1993) 62
Small plane warnings (1996) 65
Fit as a fiddle (1996) 67
Man says 'no' to dog (1994) 69
You can't go home again (1993) 72
Passing traffic (1994) 75
A museum to live by (1993) 77
Old friends and foggy nights (1995) 80
When you wish upon a star (1993) 83
Pictures 86
This winter is Jolson (1994) 90
Home on the firing range (1993) 93
Family in high places (1995) 96
Cry for me, Argentina (1997) 100

Contents, continued

Physical training at the peak (1997) 102
Grass clipping: A growth industry (1993) 105
On loan (1993) 107
We'll always have Paris (1995) 109
Gonzo with the wind (1994) 112
Twenty-five years, but who's counting (1994) 114
A silly millimeter longer (1993) 117
Nightmare on Main Street (1994) 120
Pretty Boy Floyd: Zen master (1995) 122
The brick wall (1993) 125
This above all (1995) 128
Home alone, too (1995) 131
All about the birds and the bees (1996) 134
By the silvery moon (1996) 137
My phone bill won't balance (1996) 139
Rare sightings (1997) 141
Talking to the wall: Anne Frank (1995) 144
Magic Ice (1995) 146
The loss of a lullaby (1995) 148
The wall that separates a generation (1994) 151
Summer curves (1993) 153
From here to eternity (1995) 156
Turn on, tune in, and dial (1993) 159
Water rights (1997) 162
'tis the season to be malling (1993) 165
D-Day plus fifty (1994) 167
Gordian resolutions—not (1996) 169
Reflections on a New Year's Eve (1993) 171

Introduction

I was twelve when I joined the carnival. One day, I was a small-town-America kid, the next day, I'd hitched myself to a passing show and I was the Carnie Kid, too.

When the carnival came for me, I didn't stop being small-town America. No more than I've stopped being my parent's son, or a cadet on the parade ground, or Blackie's friend. No more than I've stopped being Jody's husband or Tamara and Zev's father. No more than the artillery on the hill stops firing at me whenever I think of it. And no more than I've stopped being the Carnie Kid now that I no longer ride with the show.

The carnival pulled into town like a slow train, to pick up, discharge, and move on. That year, on schedule—on its yearly timetable—the carnival stopped in Sharon. It set up rides, took on and discharged passengers, broke down, packed up, and when it rolled again, I was part of it and it was part of me. Long before I ever wrote a column for a newspaper, I slept under the rearing hooves and watchful eyes of wildly-painted, merry-go-'round horses.

But, then, I was always watched over.

Big Daddy was born in a land ruled by a Czar and Big Mama was a subject of King Vittorio Emanuele. My parents never met them and certainly never voted for them. But Big Daddy did vote for Franklin Delano Roosevelt (Mama wasn't old enough to vote until Truman) and would have voted for Eleanor, too, if that were possible. They were part of those unpolled by the media, those who put Harry Truman in for another four years, sent the shoo-in Dewey into oblivion, and gave George Gallup the trots.

During the war, Mama set rivets at the Quincy Shipyard. Big Daddy went to India, Burma and China. He saw snake charmers and the Taj Mahal. He saw British officers step over dead and starving Indians as they strode into their officers' clubs. He told us that, in China, his Lieutenant slapped him on the back and said, Fisher, for a Jew, you're a real white man.

On Sundays and holidays, Big Mama cooked up a storm and Daddy told the same jokes we'd heard 500 times before, but they still kept us in stitches and we all joined in for the punch lines. Our dinners always included plenty of family and friends, politics, religion, and lots of laughter, with the occasional fireworks that happen when passionate people combust in the presence of brisket. My friends were always welcome at our table but God help anyone who didn't have an opinion or couldn't defend one to the death.

Big Daddy spent most of his time running his factories, or with his family, but he did spend some tiny fraction of time being a boxing manager and that was the part of him everyone knew about. How strange, he said to me, I employ hundreds of people, I love my wife and children, give to charity, and nobody cares. No newspaper shows up to write a story about those things. But when I have a fighter, everyone knows who I am.

Big Daddy took me to meet Sonny Liston at the Holiday Inn in Dedham. Liston had already lost the Heavyweight Championship of the World to Muhammad Ali in Miami. The rematch was scheduled for Boston Garden. A few days before the fight, Ali had a hernia and was rushed to Mass. General for surgery. When we arrived at the Holiday Inn, Big Daddy asked me to wait in the bar while he went off to a meeting with Sam Silverman, the Boston fight promoter. I turned to go into the bar. Sitting on a bar stool, looking at me, was a man with the saddest eyes I've ever seen. Mr. Liston? I said, and put out my hand. I remember the rough feel of his hands on mine. But his eyes had a sadness that made me want to cry. I wished him luck.

On the ride home, I told Big Daddy about the sadness. When they did fight in Lewiston, Maine, Ali knocked that sad man out soon after the fight began.

Of course, Muhammad Ali was magic—magical. He danced and shot off punches from every angle—going forward, backward, side to side. From high, from low, off balance—magical. I'd watched dozens of fighters train at Nu Nu's Gym by Boston Garden. They were mostly flat-footed, jab-jab, throw the right, tuck your chin, move forward, jab-jab, throw the right.... But Muhammad Ali was an entire carnival of punches. An Octopus ride full of punches, times ten.

Big Daddy's business partner and best friend was Mike Piccento. Mike was Rocky Marciano's uncle and our families were often together. In "Marciano's Magical Mitts," I tell about meeting the champ for the first time.

One of the first fighters Big Daddy managed was Eddie Connors from Sharon. Eddie was a welterweight. On Sunday mornings, I sat on the tailgate of our family's station wagon while Eddie did his roadwork around the lake. The night Eddie fought Tony DeMarco, the Town Selectmen canceled their regular meeting to go to the fight.

When we put our house on Marie Avenue up for sale, Eddie brought a young couple to look at it. They bought the house and we moved two streets over to Ames Court. One morning on my way to work, I picked up one of the Boston newspapers. On the front page, I saw a picture of the man who'd bought our house. In the story, they called him 'Cadillac Frank,' and described him as 'crime boss' for the Boston Mafia. Some years later, Eddie was machine gunned to death in a telephone booth on Morrissey Boulevard in Boston. My father wept.

This is a book of columns. Stories that happen to folks in a small town, and to people who live in cities, too.

I wrote a column called "Man says 'no' to dog" and, as this is a non-fiction book, every word I wrote is more-or-less true. Like *Dutch a memoir of Ronald Reagan* by Edmund Morris is true. When I wrote "Man says 'no' to dog" I did say 'no' to having a dog. I swore off dogs forever. And I meant it.

Doggie-Dog is sitting here beside me as I write. His head is on my lap. It's not easy to write with a dog's head in your lap. Jody and Zev say he's my dog and Dog does nothing to contradict them. And those same folks who now say Dog is mine once swore oaths that 'Trooper' would be theirs. I didn't believe them, but they believed themselves. (Jody believed the old woman who told her that carrying a pregnancy high meant you would have a boy—she believed that right up until the day our daughter, Tamara, was born.) Jody said Trooper's a short-haired dog and short-haired dogs don't shed. Zev said he'd feed him and take him for walks and besides, what kind of a dad denies his kid a dog?

This kind, I said.

And Jody said, look at the way he cocks his head when you speak. Have you ever seen such a face? Isn't he a beauty? Go ahead, pet him.

I kept my arms folded across my chest. I'd made up my mind a long time ago—I was off dogs forever.

An oath is an oath is an oath.

And then he hiccuped. And he hiccuped again. And before I grasped the meaning of a double dog hiccup, he threw up. And Jody gagged and said, Oh! Yech! He must be sick. And she and Zev ran out of the room. And I was left alone with a sick puppy whose last meal with his previous owner was an anchovy pizza, and here I am three-years later writing a foreword to "Man says 'no' to dog" with Dog's head lying on my lap.

Did I get snookered? My father would say, Like a piece of meat with eyes.

When people ask me what kind of dog he is, I tell them the truth. He's pure Sharon Shepherd and, although that's a pretty common breed around this town, he's a very special dog.

My life is like a carnival ride and everything in it goes around and around.

Jody's planting again. Zinnias, petunias and lettuce. This is the fifth time she's planted these same varieties this week. There is a test of wills going on in our garden. Every day Jody plants and every night the groundhogs eat. Either she's running a food pantry for woodchucks or she's hoping they'll eat so much they'll just blow the hell up. Dylan, the weathervane, says the smart money is on the rodents.

I'm lucky that Jody is as 'Jody' as she is. I could say stubborn or loving or determined or any one of a few-dozen long-stem adjectives, but they all boil down to one word and that's Jody, so that's the word I'll use. She's center star for a lot of the columns in this book and if she stopped remodeling the house, or forcing dogs on me, or trying to blow up groundhogs and the like, I'd be left with nothing much to write about.

Of course, I could always write about Big Mama. When I told her that I was working on a book, she said, Is it about me? I said that some of the stories were about her. In "Duckies and bunnies," I reveal her secret recipe for duck soup and describe a typical day in the Fisher house on Marie Avenue. In "Small plane warnings," I show how Big Mama's-mama radar can track her children to the four corners of the Earth.

A week or so ago, I was deep into a Sunday nap when the bedside phone rang. I put the phone to my ear. Hello, I mumbled, my face stuck in a pillow. Big Mama started to read. She was reading the story of her life growing up in Italy and of her coming to America. By the end of the second paragraph, I was wide awake and totally absorbed. She had never told stories like these to me before. This was a different Big Mama from the one I've known for 50-something years. This was racy, insightful stuff. And I was blown away. For half an hour, I hung on every word. And then she stopped. Why did you stop? I said.

That's enough. Now you write the rest.

Big Mama, I said, I love it. But how can I write your stories?

If I write it, said big Mama, then I'll have to say what I have to say. And you may not like what I have to say.

Wow. My mother, the female Frank McCourt.

Over the last couple of nights, I've read through the columns in this book for, perhaps, the hundredth time since I first decided to republish them more than a year ago. Last night—early this morning, really—when I finished reading, I rubbed my eyes, dropped the proof copy onto the floor beside the bed, put my glasses on the nightstand, and shut off the light, less to sleep than to lose myself among the friends who visit through these pages. And they do visit and tell me funny stories that make me laugh and make me sad and make me laugh again.

Most of these columns were first published in *The Sharon Advocate*, a newspaper you can still buy for a nickel. Back when I first started writing columns for the *Advocate,* it was a full-size, 12-page broadsheet newspaper. You could read my column and the police blotter and lots of news about the goings-on in Sharon. And all for five cents. Less than half-a-cent a page. And my columns took up slightly less than a quarter of a page. Let me get out my calculator. Hmm. Yes. And I was paid accordingly.

In many ways, columns are like snapshots of moments caught in time. One moment that didn't get caught at the time is a 1989 "Obituary" that an editor refused to publish as it involved an untimely demise under fishy circumstances. It is the only 'investigative journalism' I've ever done. I thought it appropriate to publish it now and let the chips fall where they may.

A column called "New Guys" marched around my head for a dozen years and weathered the storms of countless rewrites. I felt it was time for it to finally see the light of day. In "New Guys," I mention

Maj. who was in charge of my company of middle-school cadets when I attended New York Military Academy as an eighth and ninth grader. Major Theodore R. Dobias was one of those who kept special watch over me when I needed watching over most. I sent him an early draft of "New Guys." We visited recently, the first time in 40 years. I was humbled at the warmth that radiated from him as he recounted details about me, of our two years together and the twinkle of his eyes when he talked about things that I did as if they'd happened only that morning. The affection I took away with me after seeing the Maj. and his wife, Shirley, is matched only by the affection I feel for them.

With those exceptions, all of the columns in this book were first published in *The Sharon Advocate*, the newspaper in my hometown, Sharon, Massachusetts.

For nearly all of my life, the *Advocate* has been an important link between me and the happenings of Sharon. One day, in 1955, when we were in elementary school, Howie Rothberg and I dropped in at the *Advocate* office and asked to be cub reporters like Jimmy Olsen, the most famous cub reporter for the most famous newspaper in all the world, *The Daily Planet*. Mrs. Reeves, owner of the *Advocate*, hired us on the spot as freelancers. Within a few hours, Howie and I had returned half-a-dozen times with stories of happenings from all over town. Each time we spotted a scoop, we raced our bikes back to the office and reported to Mrs. Reeves. Each time she paid us a shiny quarter for our work. (The pay for freelancers hasn't changed much since 1955). Two dollars in, and Mrs. Reeves called it quits. It seems Howie and I had provided enough hot scoops to keep the *Advocate* in news for years. Besides, every publisher knows you have to sell a lot of nickel newspapers to make up for two dollars thrown away on free-lancers. As far as I can see, the entire newspaper business hasn't made up for those frivolous quarters right up until today.

When I left town as a 13-year-old to attend private school in New York State, my parents arranged for the *Advocate* to be sent to me there. From Cornwall-on-Hudson, I followed the comings and goings of Sharon. I faithfully read "Tess the Tattler" and learned whose relatives were in town from Carson City or Boise, who had gone to the Cape for the weekend, details of the beadwork and cross-stitching sewn on the dresses worn by the town's brides, and which six-year old had a birthday party on the backyard lawn. The *Advocate* informed me of births and deaths in my hometown. I eagerly read the school menu to see when my former schoolmates would be blessed with fricassee hamburger on mashed potato—I can taste that culinary delight to this day. And to this day, I don't know who ate the chopped-ham-and-relish on buttered-bread sandwiches. But far and away my favorite part of the *Advocate* was the "Police Blotter as reported by Bernice Leonard."

Those special words, 'as reported by,' make all the difference in the world between the police blotters of today and the ones I loved back in the 1950s and for years after.

Each week, Mrs. Leonard went to the police station and hand-copied selected entries from the weekly log. By the time those entries were set in lead and printed in the paper, many had a wry quip or kicker attached that fantasized what the officers had encountered when they answered a call. Mrs. Leonard's "Police Blotter" was the part of the *Advocate* that Sharonites turned to first when they read their town's news.

Even in Cornwall, at New York Military Academy, groups of cadets would read aloud from Mrs. Leonard's accounts of the Sharon police who served and protected my hamlet of 5000 souls. Back then, it all seemed pretty natural to me that kids who came from all over the United States and from countries as far away as Saudi Arabia and Venezuela, Dubai, and El Salvador, and kids who would never be able to return to their homes in the cities and towns of Castro's Cuba, all found warmth and humor in Mrs. Leonard's accounts of the Sharon Police Department.

In military school, watching my friends read Mrs. Leonard's columns, I saw how writing, tinged with humor, could transcend countries and continents and make Sharon a hometown for kids from almost everywhere.

Thirty years later, when I started writing columns for the *Advocate*, it was a joy to appear in the same paper with Bernice Leonard.

In 1987, the *Advocate* moved from its long-time home at 66 South Main Street (where the CVS is now) across the street to 21 South Main, the Florence Kates building, beside the barn I rented from Florence. Around that time, I wrote a letter to the editor about a remodeling project that had turned Post Office Square into a gigantic mud pond. My barn had no bathroom or running water, and, as Florence was landlord for both buildings, I shared facilities in the main building with the *Advocate* staff. On one of my forays to visit the porcelain, I stuck my head into the newspaper office to see what was going on there. Someone asked if I was the writer of the mud-pond letter and would I like to submit some freelance columns to the paper. That was the start of it.

Like the carnival come to town, the coincidence of a letter to the editor, the *Advocate's* move, and a lack of plumbing set me on another unexpected course.

From time to time, when there was space to fill in the editorial section of the paper, Stuart Green published one of my columns under the tag, "A View From A Barn." A half dozen or so had run when Stuart, the *Advocate's* managing editor, and I were both at a retirement party for Harold Lew, cantor of Temple Israel. I had written a column about the Cantor that appeared in that week's edition. Quite a few people attended the party, and quite a few of them approached Stuart or me to comment favorably on what I'd been writing and on what I'd said about the Cantor. I don't know which of us was more startled by the reaction, but that night I became a regular columnist in *The Sharon Advocate*.

Some weeks earlier, Pat Goudey, an *Advocate* reporter, appeared at my barn. Let me see what you're writing, she demanded. I had never met Pat before but I handed her the column I'd just finished. She picked up a pen and started to cross out words, circle others, and put giant question marks all over the page. Trust your reader, she said as she drew lines through my words. You have to trust more. I grabbed the column out of her hand and angrily started to read. The voice was mine, the words were mine, but there were fewer of them and what remained was stronger for the pruning. It was like she'd pulled the suckers off my prized tomato plant.

I didn't know it, but after one or two of my columns had run in the paper, Pat began lobbying Stuart and Melody Howard, the editor of the *Advocate*, to make a regular place for me in the paper. She had decided to watch over this wild teller of Sharon tales, and make him a writer, t'boot.

My *Advocate* columns became a series of short stories about a Sharon family. And through all the years, Pat Goudey continues to hack and slash at my words.

For this first volume of *The Carnie Kid tells all*, Pat and I selected columns that cover the entire span of years that I wrote for *The Sharon Advocate*. From more than 300 columns, we selected 64 that we love and believe tell the story of the world as the Carnie Kid finds it. Each column was fought over and edited, and fought over and edited, and reedited, again. I hope you'll like them even more this time around.

Yes it's true, my wife, Jody, and I met in the School Street School on our first day of kindergarten nearly 50-years ago and only 50 yards from where we live today. Jody has been a wonderful sport letting me use the stories of our life together as fair game for my columns. Our daughter, Tamara, our son, Zev, and my mother, Big Mama Fisher, have let me play with their idiosyncrasies with remarkable forbearance and good nature. I once told Zev that he couldn't have an advance on his allowance until he mowed the lawn. Zev was in a rush to get out the door to meet up with his friends. Sure, Dad, for you, I'm only a character in your column. It wasn't true. It isn't true. Zev is a character in his own right. And I gave him the money anyway.

Columnists are dangerous to be around. You never know when some comment you make, some quirk you have, even a description of how you chew your food, will find its way into thousands of homes. I've been blessed with wonderful friends who I've exploited shamelessly for the readers of *The Sharon Advocate*.

Anyone who writes knows what a good animal story can do for a writer and I've had a menagerie of well-loved, eccentric multi-leggeds who have taken over my house, my life, and of course, my column. From Blackie, Oreo, Pretty Boy Floyd, Gypsie, Cookie, Fluffy, right on through to Tom Quin's dog, Whatsizname. Only our dog, Trooper—his head is still in my lap—came along too late to be included in a column for the *Advocate*. One pet—more a friend, really—Dylan, the copper weathervane who lives in the cupola on the roof of my house, continues to be one of my closest advisors and confidants.

The editors of *The Sharon Advocate*, Melody Howard, Stuart Green, Tom Glynn, and of course Pat Goudey, are very special people who demonstrated the hard work, dedication, and integrity found in local newspapering. My friend, Rhonda Sugarman, office manager at the paper, did a last read for me before my columns hit the presses and, on more than one occasion, Rhonda saved me from an embarrassing Friday morning typo. Fred Neithold made the newspaper rounds to the stores and provided me with first reactions each time my column appeared.

One of the columns included in this collection, "New years, old stories," aired on WBUR's *Morning Edition*. Eve Epstein, the program's Editor called to make arrangements for me to read it on the air.

When I submitted the column, it hadn't occurred to me that I'd be the one to actually read the piece aloud. The machinations we went through to make my voice sing-song up and down to give it expression were extremely painful. In the end, I was spliced together and digitally remastered. For two-and-a-half minutes of airtime, I spent more than an hour at the microphone and a full week gargling with hot water and asprin to make my throat normal again.

I was asleep and missed the piece when it first aired at 6:30 in the morning. A lot of people did hear it, though. My phone started ringing at 6:32:31 so I was wide awake for the 8:30 rerun. I never knew so many people stayed awake all night and right into the morning like that.

Billy Peters is a special friend who appears in many of my stories. I've known Billy for nearly all of my life. We grew up together in Sharon, walked the same streets, swam in the lake, played fort together. He ate dinner at my house almost every night. Although, you won't find his name on any street list, I can assure you that you've walked by his house, run into him up town, gone to school with him, seen him shagging flies or rooting for his kids down at the field. I run into Billy everywhere I go. And I'm certain that if I pointed him out to you, you'd know him at once.

In view of the recent plagiarism scandals at the *Boston Globe*, let me assure you that the only unattributed lifts in my columns are the spelling. Nearly every word of spelling I've ever published was abducted from brains other than my own.

Once, a long time ago, a carnival came to Sharon. The rides clanked and whirred. Children laughed and screamed while clutches, gears, and mechanical arms rocked and tossed them them this way and that. Midnight came. The fairway went dark. The carnies packed up the trucks and rolled into the night.

For the Carnie Kid, that day and forever after brought highways full of new adventures. But from time to time when the road forked, and the map proved inadequate to get the show to the next booking, at times like those, the Kid found that there are people in the land who will step forward to keep a show on track. Dov and Alina Kentof, Lenny Pazol, Michael Bearse, Owen Surman, and Lillian Krovitsky each kept watch over the Carnie Kid when the road ahead turned perilous. Although there are no stories about them in this volume, each of them has made the Carnival run.

For the readers of *The Sharon Advocate* who were so kind to me and my column over the years, and to those of you now reading them for the first time, I hope you enjoy this volume. I certainly loved writing these columns, and revisiting them for this book has only added to the pleasure.

Zev tells me that a carnival is pulling in up by the Sacred Heart field. If I hurry, perhaps I can watch the crew setting up the Wheel and take a few turns on the 'Jenny,' to whisper again with wild-eyed horses like those who watched over me as I slept when I was a 12-year-old Carnie Kid in need of watching over.

Ilan Fisher
Summer, 2001

Apologia

My mother wanted this book to be a novel. I told her it's a book of columns. I explained that, unlike columns, novels take years to write. I told her that the characters in a novel bore into your brain through your eyes and set up housekeeping in your mushy, green gray-matter. They don't pay rent and they demand you eavesdrop on them and faithfully record each ooh and aah on paper as they conspire, fight, and make torrid love on every cranial outcrop you possess. And heaven forbid you turn away for a moment, one or another will stab a manicured nail right into your auditory canal and throw a screeching fit until you pay close attention to what she's about, even when you have pressing things of your own to attend to. And you're forced to scream, Get out of my head and get a life; and then this character—this person you invented—in her best soft-sexy voice, whispers that you are her life, Honey, so hit the damn keyboard.

I've tried writing novels and I can tell you, writing novels is worse than owning a dog. Being a novelist is like being a columnist whose mother phoned for the tenth time this morning to ask if this book isn't really going to be a novel.

I'm sorry, Ma. It's only a book of columns.

The first Thanksgiving ever

(1992)

Mama Fisher knew she was going into labor. She had felt it most of the day. She spoke with Emma, the lady who lived next door, then packed the things she would need for the hospital in a small suitcase that she put in the bedroom closet.

She opened the icebox. There was still plenty of ice in the compartment and the turkey felt fine. She would stuff it and put it in the oven at dawn, then she would have the baby.

Big Daddy arrived home from work after dark, but she decided it was too early to tell him. She had never had a child before and didn't want to excite him in case she was mistaken.

By ten o'clock that night the labor still hadn't taken on a regular pattern. Mama went to bed thinking of the things she had to do in the morning. An hour later, she called out to Big Daddy.

"My water's broken," she said.

The only thing Big Daddy knew less about than babies was the process for having babies. Big Mama's declaration might well have been almost any collection of words. He understood her to mean that she had taken a hot water bottle to bed and had rolled over onto it, causing it to burst. Even though Big Mama was nearing the end of her pregnancy, he was surprised her weight could split a hot water bottle.

"Are you sure you put the plug in right?" he asked.

Big Mama looked at him strangely. "I broke my water," she said. "The things are in the closet." She started to get out of bed.

Big Daddy went to the dresser to get a change of sheets.

"There is a suitcase in the closet." Big Mama pointed toward the closet door with some urgency.

By this time, Big Daddy had the drawer open and the sheets were in his hand.

"The suitcase is in the closet."

"I have dry sheets." He held the sheets out in front of him, hoping she would take them and make the bed.

"We don't have time to change the bed. We have to call a cab and get to the hospital now. I've broken my water."

Big Daddy stood with the sheets in his hand and it struck him that something was going on that he wasn't quite comprehending. He pulled back the bed covers. No hot water bottle was in sight. "Where's the hot water bottle?" he asked, his voice flattening to a hoarse rasp as he tried to make sense of wet sheets and no bottle.

"Call the cab," Big Mama ordered as she struggled into her dress. "I'll get the suitcase myself."

The taxi arrived. Big Daddy explained to the driver that they were about to have a baby. "Get us to the hospital fast."

It had begun to snow. Heavy, wet flakes—more rain than snow—as the cab sped toward Booth Memorial Hospital.

Big Daddy attempted to take control. "Everything is going to be all right," he said. He still wasn't certain he understood what had transpired in the bedroom, but it seemed as if Big Mama knew, so he felt somewhat reassured.

Bang! They were thrown into the air. The seat jogged up and down. The taxi thumped along to a stop. They had blown a tire.

It was late, past midnight, and Big Mama's labor was now regular and strong. Big Daddy faced the prospect of assisting with life's unknowns on a pitch-black Boston street.

Car lights appeared in the distance. Big Daddy jumped out of the cab and straddled the roadway, frantically waving his arms over his head. The oncoming taxi was forced to stop to avoid hitting him. Angrily, the cabby rolled down his window.

Big Daddy explained the predicament. The driver pointed to his passenger in the back of the cab. "I'd be glad to take you, Mack, but it's his cab."

The passenger was on his way home from a night spot and a Thanksgiving eve celebration. He struggled to pull himself upright and agreed to allow the couple to divert his cab to Booth Memorial. He moved up to the front seat.

Big Mama needed most of the back seat to find a comfortable position.

Heavy, wet snow was falling as the cab pulled up to the hospital. The driver and Big Daddy helped Big Mama inside where nurses quickly took over.

Big Daddy returned to the cab and retrieved the suitcase. He took a twenty-dollar bill from his pocket and tried to give it to the passenger. The benefactor had recovered a flask from his overcoat and was celebrating his relief from the anxious responsibility he had assumed by gulping liquid heart-rate relaxer.

Seeing the bill in Big Daddy's hand, the man magnanimously waved it away. In slurred but deliberate speech, he declared, "Sir, this baby's on me," and saluted the hapless husband with a flourish of his flask before returning it to his lips.

Despite its early antics, the baby fought hard to keep its home of nine months. Holding on until dawn, he would have liked to have slept in that morning, but somehow the tug of the passing moon and the allure of the rising sun declared that, on this morning, he was due for a very big wake up call.

Big Mama was unconscious as I entered the world. And Big Daddy was nowhere in sight.

I distinctly remember hearing the exhausted doctor tell the nurse. "Thank God that's over. I have to get home. It's Thanksgiving."

As far as I know, it was the first Thanksgiving ever.

Duckies and bunnies

(1994)

PROLOGUE: On a crisp spring morning, Mother Duck led her troop of hatchlings single-file through the woods, carefully negotiating the dense underbrush as she went. She heard a cry from behind her. One of her troop had stumbled and was caught in a tangle of wild thicket. She signaled him to be silent and to rejoin the line.

Struggling to obey, the duckling tried to push his way free by flapping his wings. The thicket seemed to reach up and grab him, holding his small, thrashing body suspended. He cried out again for his mother. Angrily, she ordered silence. Fearing his cries would endanger the entire brood, she closed ranks and marched her family away, abandoning the fettered offspring to his fate.

The Fisher house on Marie Avenue was often home to a menagerie of multi-legged residents. Animals that didn't show up at the kitchen door for a quickie 'lunch and lap' were either impervious to the aromas of Mama Fisher's famous animal cuisine or dead, and sometimes, even the dead made an appearance 'post mortem,' brought in by a Fisher kid for attempted resuscitation by Mama Fisher. No animal was considered truly dead until Mama herself pronounced it so. So, it was business as usual when my sister Paula brought the tiny, half-dead duckling home to Mama for the laying on of hands.

What a relief. Baby duck rescued from the brink, delivered into the warm healing presence at Mama Fisher's hearth.

But Paula wasn't the first Fisher to bring an injured animal into Mama's kitchen that day. Blackie, the dog, had preceded her by at least an hour, and it was Blackie's find that Big Mama was tending to at that very moment.

Blackie placed the baby rabbit at Mama's feet. The stunned creature lay there for the time it took Big Mama to put the dog out, then it jumped up and ran behind the stove. No amount of cooing or coaxing could dislodge the quivering bunny from his refuge. Big, black retriever dogs and humans were monsters this baby bunny never wanted to meet again. Undeterred, Mama Fisher went to the closet and took out the vacuum cleaner. She slipped a sock over the nozzle and slid it under the stove and up against the rabbit. She flipped the switch and—pop—Big Mama had him, one baby bunny in a sock.

After bagging the big game, Mama handed him to little brother David and turned her attention to the duckling. Following a thorough examination, she pronounced him intact and hungry. She pulled a few delicacies from the refrigerator that she knew would appeal to a baby duck and placed them in her mouth. She chewed them to a paste that she forced down the duck's bill. A large, shallow pan was filled with warm water and the duckling hoarsely peep-quacked approval for his full tummy and private pool.

Little David hugged the bunny in his arms. He refused to release it until Big Mama promised she would bring it to school the next day for show-and-tell. Mama promised. But the immediate problem was how to feed the fur ball. She drove to the Heights Plaza and the toy store to buy a doll's bottle. Once back home, she concocted a special liquid formula and the bunny started to drink, his front paws holding the bottle as he greedily slurped his meal.

Night settled over 14 Marie Avenue. Mama and Papa Fisher were in their bed. The three Fisher kids were settled in, with Blackie and me sharing the same pillow. In the back hall, with the boots and the trash bag, were the two new Fisher babies—the ducky and the bunny.

Morning came and, as usual, the Fisher kids were going to be late for school. In a flurry, they were pushed out the door toward their various destinations. Big Mama had to promise David she wouldn't forget to bring his bunny in to show his classmates.

Once the kids were out the front door, Mama turned her attention to the back hall. The duckling had hopped into his water pan, but the bunny was nowhere to be seen. Mama decided to feed the duck first and look for the rabbit after. When she went to scoop the duckling from the pan,.she found the surface of the water turned to ice and the duck—stuck.

Mama Fisher screamed a word she would only use in great panic. She ran and turned on the stove. Placing the pan—duck and all—on the burner, she watched the ice melt away. At exactly the right instant, she snatched the former ducksickle from the soup. "Peep-Quack!" he exclaimed over and over as he marched around the kitchen floor, "Peep-Quack!"

Mama chewed up some ducky breakfast and pushed it down his throat. In between swallows, he looked at her and repeated, "Peep-Quack!" She placed the pan on the floor, but he was having none of it and scampered under the kitchen table.

A close call.

Now, it was time to feed the rabbit and get him over to the Heights Elementary School. Mama looked in the back hall but he was still nowhere in sight. She had been careful to close the door, so he couldn't have escaped outside or into the kitchen. She looked in each of the boots that lay in a pile—no rabbit. The milkman hadn't come that day, but she checked the milkbox anyway. She looked behind the brown-paper trash bag and inside the bag, too.

Then something caught her eye. Movement in a discarded marsh-mallow jar? "Oh, no," she groaned as she carried the jar to the sink. Carefully covering the disposal, she shook the jar. The rabbit was stuck fast. She gently tried to pry him loose with a wooden spoon but he was gooed in tight. She dribbled warm water over his head and slowly sloshed the watery marshmallow around and around. Finally, the bunny wiggled his way free. With a plop and a splash, he was in the sink.

Working rapidly, with painstaking care, Mama washed the marsh-mallow from the mellow fellow's fur. He looked and acted every bit the drowned bunny. She sat by the fireplace, wrapped him in a towel, and dried him until his fur fluffed and his ears perked. Big Mama knew he was all right when he wrapped his paws around the doll's bottle and he sucked down a double dose of formula. Then it was off to David's school.

By the end of the summer, we were able to introduce our duck into the Marie Avenue swamp where some other ducks lived. In fact, they may have been members of his natural family, although he was clearly the largest and best looking of the lot, having been raised on Big

Mama's special recipes. When the season turned, he did what we feared and hoped he'd do. He went south and joined the circus. And the rabbit? Well, it turned out he had a mother and some brothers and sisters that Blackie sniffed out the day after the great marshmallow adventure. We returned the bunny to his burrow and watched with binoculars. His mother sniffed him over, then leapt into the air. Hopping and zigzagging as fast as she could, she made for the woods. Then, just as suddenly, she came back and nuzzled his fur with her nose. Either she recognized him as one of her own or she'd discovered the delightful taste of marshmallow and just wanted to keep him around.

No free ride

(1989)

Zap! There went the 1980s.

Billy Peters caught a glimpse of the 90s the other day—gridlock in front of the Post Office. I don't think Billy could have understood the concept of gridlock in Sharon back when he bought his first car.

It was a time when a Mustang was only a horse, Omega a Greek symbol, Stingray an ugly fish, GTO, RX7, and 450 SL just random letters and numbers.

Back then, in the Muranos' Marie Avenue driveway, Richie Murano and Jeff Glover from Harold Street were working on a 'hot rod'—a mid-1930s Ford with a roll bar and an exposed engine. Richie and his friends worked on this car with gusto. They were always covered with grease, had wrenches in their hands, were rolling under or out from under the car. They'd tighten and loosen and weld and, every once in a while, they would push their car into the road, roll it a little, pop the clutch, and off they'd go—black smoke and roaring sound pouring from the mufflerless tailpipe as they headed off around the block to test their latest additions and adjustments.

These were the old guys on the block, maybe 15 or 16 years old. The younger kids watched them drive by and desperately wanted a car of their own.

As luck would have it, Mr. Haverly, who lived at the corner of Gunhouse and Marie, had two cars for sale in his yard—a 1949 Chevrolet and a '48 Studebaker.

Without consulting his parents, 13-year-old Billy Peters went up, talked to Mr. Haverly, and bought a car. First, he walked around both cars, kicked the tires, opened the hoods to view the incomprehensible wires, carburetors and engine shapes, and then, after listening to a description of the differences between 'flat-head' and 'L-head' engines, bought the Chevrolet. It wasn't that one car ran better than the other or the prices were any different—the choice boiled down to names. 'Studebaker' grates on the ear and sounds like some disgusting Martian vegetable. The name is packed with ugly consonant sounds like the word 'garbage' and, when taken all together, translated to Billy as grinding gears and hard to drive. So, he dug into his pocket, paid out his $15, and Mr. Haverly delivered the sweet-sounding Chevy to its new home at 14 Marie Avenue.

Billy's parents talked it over, then laid down the ground rules. The gang could work on the car in the driveway, but under no circumstances was it to be on the road. The conditions were readily accepted, the group of 13-year-old whiffle cuts bobbing their heads in assent.

For the first few days, they took turns pushing the starter button, putting the shift lever into gear, letting up on the clutch, and backing up the five feet to the road's edge, and then fighting over who would drive the return trip. Then, an ominous event occurred—the battery went dead.

Billy went down to talk to Richie Murano, who explained the process of popping the clutch to get the car running. The only problem was the car needed to be rolling for the method to work.

As everyone knows, in front of 14 Marie Avenue, there's a hill. At the first opportunity, when Billy's parents were away from the house, the gang gathered to push the Chevy to the top of the hill. A 1949 Chevrolet was made of steel—no plastic or alloy or synthetic anything—just steel and lots of it.

With their backs pressed against the front bumper, their sneakers slipping on the asphalt, the gang strained the Chevrolet up the hill. At the top, they rushed to get behind the car and shoved as hard as they could in the opposite direction. The Chevy started downhill. As it picked up speed, everyone jumped inside.

Billy stepped on the clutch and moved the shift lever into second gear. He braced himself and slipped his foot from the pedal. The clutch popped, the car jerked—nothing happened. He tried again. The tires grabbed and squealed but, again, no start. The car was slowly rolling toward a stop. Billy looked down at the key. It was off. Quickly, he flipped it on and popped the clutch for a third time.

The engine screamed, then roared like a lion.

The car, already in second gear, shot off down the street. Billy made the turn onto Gertrude Ave, then Harold Street. He shifted into third, the car bucked but, at those speeds, it didn't stall. Around and around the block the Chevy and its crew rode. With growing confidence, Billy changed direction, turned left onto Harold Street, then Ames, and out onto Main Street.

Main Street—Sharon's superhighway.

Before he knew it, Billy was going too fast for a successful turn back onto Gertrude Ave. So with a hard swallow and some testing of the brakes, he drove past the DPW garage and made the left onto Gunhouse. Shifting through the gears, heart racing, he arrived back home on Marie Avenue and the safety of his driveway.

That whole summer, the gang pretended to work on the Chevy, even painting it, applying the green, interior house paint with brushes. Billy, who had no interest in auto mechanics at all, always carried an assortment of tools in hand as he climbed over and slid under or out from under the Chevy, anticipating the time when both his parents would be gone from the house. Then push, push, push, the Chevy went up the hill, started rolling down, and—screech—the gang was off exploring the far side of the Lake, driving through the trails behind the Sacred Heart School. And perhaps, once in a week, the gang dared a pass Uptown—four or five stubble-headed 13-year-olds in a brush-painted, green Chevy driving through the Square.

When fall turned to winter, Billy's parents called Mr. Biondi, the junk man. He came and hauled the Chevy away and paid Billy $10 for it, too. Things were like that then, no gridlock on the horizon and, for $5, a kid could drive a Chevy all summer long.

Kindergarten chemistry
(1994)

'Lovely New England farmhouse fixer-upper. Caveat emptor and e pluribus unum. Let the buyer beware and bring lots of bucks.'

Twenty-two years after reading the real-estate advertisement, and forty very-odd years after seeing the old house for the first time, the truth of those words is still sinking in.

My wife Jody is wallpapering our son Zev's room. Jody is a great wallpaperer. She should be, she's had lots of practice and a fair amount of it in Zev's room.

Zev's room overlooks the school administration building, which was once a high school, an elementary school, and, on my first day in the Sharon school system, the town's centralized kindergarten. There were two classrooms in the old school, Mrs. Hamer's and Miss Harris's. By the end of my first week there, I had met all the important five-year-old Sharonites of my day and one in particular who would prove especially significant in my future.

That first night at the dinner table, my parents wanted to know all about school. I told them about coloring and finger painting, the two recess periods, how the bathroom was called the boy's lab'ratory. I explained about opening exercises, which were not exercises at all, but listening to Miss Harris read from the Bible, and how we put our hands over our hearts to pledge allegiance to one nation, invisible.

I told them a lot, but I didn't tell them about the most important thing I had learned on that first day of kindergarten.

I recall seeing her at early recess. She was hanging upside-down by her knees from the jungle gym, arms swinging downward, her dark hair almost touching the ground. Back in class, I couldn't take my eyes off her. We sat semi-circle on the wood floor. She sat with a group of girls across from me. Sometimes she giggled and laughed and her wide, dark eyes twinkled. Watching her, I had to laugh, too.

The boy sitting next to me drew a heart in the air with his fingers. My face flushed. The girl looked at me, then clasped her hands over her mouth, trying to muffle a giggle. I perspired.

Miss Harris called on me and asked if everything was all right. Every girl but one laughed out loud. Miss Harris told me to pay more attention to class and less to a certain young lady. The whole class burst into squeals of laughter, those not rolling on the floor were drawing heart shapes in the air. I dropped my gaze to my sneakers. Stealing a glance across the room, I couldn't see her face, only the top of her head and her dark brown hair.

Miss Harris restored order and I kept my eyes front.

At second recess, I looked to where the girls were playing. She was standing by herself. I started toward her. She moved to the other side of a giant oak and told me to leave her alone. She was wearing a name tag and I would have read her name had I known how to read, but it was only the first day of kindergarten and I was months away from reading.

Recess ended. We met in the corridor outside the classroom. "What's your name?" I asked.

She frowned. "That was terrible." she said.

I agreed, being laughed at had been awful.

"Why were you looking at me?" she asked.

"I saw you on the jungle gym. Can I marry you?"

The frown broke and the twinkle I had seen before lit in her eyes. She turned to go back into the classroom. Then, at the door, she stopped and turned back toward me. "Yes," she said.

"What's your name?"

"Jody."

We met after school and sat on top of the jungle gym looking at the old weathered farmhouse next door.

"When we get married, do you want to live in a house like that one?" she asked.

"No. I want a nice new one."

She pressed my hand. "Well," she said. "We don't have to decide right now." Her eyes were laughing again.

That night at dinner, I told my parents all about my first day in kindergarten. Everything, that is, except the name of the girl I had met, the girl I was going to marry.

Next week, when all of Sharon's kindergartens are reunified, this time in a wing at the high school, who can predict what special chemistry will be produced in those classrooms, playgrounds, and lab'ratories?

In the catbird seat
(1990)

Oreo could have been a skunk had her white stripe run down her back instead of her belly. But it doesn't and she's Zev's kitten.

Last night, when I let Oreo out to play, giant white flakes fell from the sky. Main Street shimmered with that mix of snow and diffused light that we wait for in Sharon. Shot with color film, the world beyond my door would still develop as a photograph in black-and-white. In that light, the maple trees that line my drive appear dark and ominous. They reach eerily through the night with bony, black boughs top-shaded in pure white snow. The entire scene floats on a canvas of gray mist.

At one o'clock in the morning, standing at my front door in my underwear, I whistled for Zev's kitten to return home. The street in front of my house was as beautiful and as silent as I've ever known it. A single line of paw prints trailed down the steps from the porch. Aside from prints, the snow was pure and unmarked.

Night is the nicest time to watch snowfall. Late at night, when the town is asleep and only the light of street lamps reflects off the snow and streaks the mist. The sound of my whistle floated through the heavy air and I listened for Oreo's pads on the snow. I listened but there was only the hanging wet silence that must have embraced Sharon for thousands of years on such snowy nights.

I stood at the door for some long minutes and whistled into the silence, the while storing images with my senses for my memory scrapbook. I find that nothing quite matches standing in a doorway on Main Street in underwear, whistling for a kitten, to fix a beautiful night forever in my mind.

I whistled into the night and was answered by a frightened, muffled mew. I whistled again. Once more, the answer was a plea.

Quickly clothed, I was out the door, my boots kicking up and crushing down miniature snowmen as I ran.

I called her name and Oreo called back. Then I spotted her, twenty feet up in a maple tree, clinging to a nook and braced between a branch and the giant trunk—stuck and afraid.

I stood back and looked at the giant black tree against the sky. All its branches were topped in white. Only one thing was out of place, upside down—a tiny incongruity in an otherwise perfect winter-night scene—a black kitten with its white stripe on the bottom, up in a tree, shaking like a leaf.

"Come on, Oreo," I prodded, "Kittens can climb down trees."

Oreo shifted position. Her body shook on wobbly legs. She looked down at me and sounded a plaintive call that sounded remarkably like, "Do something, Ilan."

I ran for the extension ladder and set it against a bough. As I tested the footing, a blob of wet snow shook loose from the branch. Its impact on the ground wasn't the only impression it made when it fell. I raced up the ladder and scooped the kitten from her perch.

The kitten and I sat next to each other on the front steps. Before going to bed, I needed to capture a last memory of this wintry night. On the ladder, I hadn't thought to look around. I supposed that Oreo hadn't appreciated much either. The scene on Main Street was back in harmony with nature. The faint street lamps gave texture to the mist. The black silhouettes had proper white stripes of snow on top where they belonged.

I stroked the kitten and felt a purr in return. Had I looked down at Zev's Oreo, the kitten who is marked like a skunk turned upside-down, I might have seen her staring at a branch way up in the highest maple, twitching her whiskers and flicking her tail from side to side.

Marciano's magical mitts

(1993)

Growing up in the Fisher household on Marie Avenue and Ames Court in the 1950s and '60s was like being a moth living on a cool florescent bulb. Bright excitement was always at hand though no fire could singe your wings.

The house was visited by a cast of characters that included United States Senators, presidential advisors, sports figures, newspapermen, boxers, promoters, garmentos, bank-robbers, cops, Mafiosi, lawyers, pets, kids, and wild animals. Every variety of exotica a kid could wish for, and a few extras tossed in, passed through the Fisher house to jawbone with Big Daddy and eat Mama's famous food. And, for this twelve-year-old Fisher kid, there appeared one day, the greatest fighter who ever put on the gloves.

I was home alone at the house on Marie Avenue. There was a knock at the door. When I answered it, a giant man filled the entryway. "Murray's kid?" the man said.

I nodded.

"I have a few calls to make," he said. He walked past me into the kitchen, sat down at the table, and reached for the black, rotary-dial telephone.

It was a reach I will never forget.

His right hand surrounded and engulfed the entire telephone. This was no Princess phone or compact portable toy of today, but a circa-1958, full-size, squarish, black table phone big enough to ring with real bells. A telephone's telephone. And it disappeared—swallowed up body, soul, and receiver—inside the most gigantic mitt of a right hand that ever existed on Planet Earth.

I didn't need the champ to introduce himself at the door. I guess he didn't think so, either. If I had any doubt about the identity of the giant sitting at our kitchen table making telephone calls, I had only to look at that phone-munching right hand to know that this mitt belonged to Rocky Marciano. The very hand that had defeated 49 of 49 opponents, 43 by knock-out, had now retired undefeated to my kitchen to maul the telephone.

While one giant hand swallowed up the phone, the other was at his face. No doubt ready to block against an overhand right.

I stood by the table listening to his distinctively-pitched Brockton accent. There was great respect in my house for fighters for theirs, we knew, was a world where, after all the celebration and hoopla of the last success faded, it was the fighter alone who would again climb into the ring and pit his courage, stamina, and skill against another man wanting to knock him unconscious, to use him as a stepping stone to money and success, to punch through him to attain the American dream, or, in the case of Rocky, take his title and supplant him in history.

Rocky was a tactical fighter, master of a single, perfect fight strategy—the feeding shark—constantly move forward, relentlessly throw punches. In the Rocky strategy, neither the beauty of the delivery nor the punches' destination on the foe's body mattered. Dozens, hundreds of shots to an opponent's ribs and arms, would prove just as lethal as a solid shot to the head when, in later rounds, the adversary could no longer breathe or lift his gloves to defend himself from the barrage of bombs that would eventually drop him to the canvas.

The hands, the honed offense, were in well-deserved retirement after years of constant motion, training regimens, self denial, heavy bags, speed bags, sparring partners, punctuated 49 times by trial in the ring. This man had willed himself champion of the world. He permitted no distractions from that goal. No opponent stood in the way of his determination to win. And nothing stood in the way of those hands that led the attack.

I grew up around boxers, gyms, Rocky's family and entourage. My father, Murray Fisher, and Rocky's uncle, Mike Piccento, were best friends, business partners, fight managers, and boxing-trivia devotees. By the time I was face-to-face with the champ at our front door, I had seen every Marciano fight available on film, some dozens of times.

Sometimes, former Marciano corner men like old Charlie Goldman, who had more than three hundred fights himself, or Ali Colombo would be with my father training a fighter or at a gathering of the clan for a meal. But for one reason or another, the day he came to use our phone was the first time I'd actually seen the champ himself.

Rocky died 23 years ago in a plane crash. He holds a unique place in boxing history—the only Heavyweight Champion of the World to retire undefeated in his professional boxing career.

A lot has been written these past weeks about the champion who, had he lived, would have been age 70 on September 1. For me the most enduring image of Rocky Marciano has always been the memory of the magical hands that fought their way to glory and made our telephone disappear.

Ellis: island in the sun
(1990)

My brother bought a plaque on the Immigrant's Wall at Ellis Island to honor our father's journey from a small village in Russia/Poland to life here in Sharon, America.

The village was called Horodok. My Daughter, Tamara, and I spent some time at the Harvard University Library this summer trying to locate Horodok on the map, but we ran into difficulty as Horodok (sometimes spelled Gorodok) apparently means 'small village' in Russian, and the present Russian-Polish border is littered with Horodoks of both spellings.

My grandfather left for the United States before my father was born. Eight years would pass before father and son would meet for the first time. Those waiting in Europe saw World War I, displacement, death, and hunger. In that part of the world, national borders traveled while people stayed at home. Thus, my grandfather emigrated from Russia, while my grandmother and their two sons emigrated from that same village as Polish nationals eight years later.

At the Fisher house on Marie Avenue, dinner always included a loaf of fresh rye bread on the table. How many times I remember my father picking up a piece of the bread, looking at it, and telling us that, as a child, he often dreamed of having a crust of bread to eat just for himself, preferably a crust rubbed with garlic.

For the eight-year-old, Ellis Island was the gateway to a life free from hunger, gateway to a life undreamed of even by his older brother and mother. Undreamed of because, in the world they came from, what lay on this side of the Statue of Liberty was unimaginable.

As I look at their passport photo, the mother and the two boys wearing Russian-style side-button shirts, I imagine their trip to a new world, a new life, and the port of entry—Ellis Island.

They came by boat, with others like themselves, cramped far below decks—steerage class. A mother and her children. Twentieth century explorers from 17th century villages.

The rolling sea made them sick. Memories of the past and the unknowns of the future intertwined and made them sick. And the smell of sickness all around made them sick. They were eyes quietly watching, ears listening, inhaling the minimum necessary to sustain life—yet, enough to exchange the familiar smell of the village for the unfamiliar air of the unknown.

The ones with children, like my grandmother, were the lucky ones; jeopardy bred opportunity. The children had to move around, to explore, to go to the bathroom, and the parent had to watch over them. In the beginning, children could be kept close with a look, a soft word, a slight reproach. But as time passed, a parent had to raise her voice, to move a limb and, finally, foray out of the past to follow and shield her children from the dangers of the unknown.

The children became the North Star, the beacon to follow through the dangerous pathways of rusted, creaking steel corridors until they led the way to the deck, the sky, and the sunlight.

Grandmother was a tall woman for her time, perhaps five-foot-eight. She was muscular, lean, and strong. Her hair had been cut short for the journey and its length accented her sharp nose and high forehead. Her skin was tight and unwrinkled. Her carriage straight. Her eyes were brown, mother's eyes, soft yet alert, like those of a mother lioness.

From the photograph, Grandmother's eyes stand as gateway to her soul, the right eye looking straight into the camera. The family historian can read determination in that eye, the will and resolve to push ahead, to face the unknown and master it. The left eye looked equally straight into the lens, although with a portion of the lid tucked ever so slightly, forming a tiny veil—enough of a veil to suggest Bedouin women screening their skin from the sun and the gaze of strangers. In the desert, rules are strict. Only the most intimate may look, and the most perceptive, see. Is something there, some long-ago connection with the desert?

The tuck could suggest 'East.' The remnant of some far-removed gene? What can we conjure up? A slow-moving gene that made its way, generation-by-generation, through the Caucasus, the Urals, Siberia, Manchuria? Or did it ride with the great horde, directly and suddenly passing into Europe with the thrusting army of Genghis Khan?

She, too, traveled west, this mother with her two cubs in tow. The younger, the hellion, my father, had to be watched at all times. But the older was a help and he kept his brother from trouble by a natural authority and maturity greater than their two-year difference in age would suggest. His was an authority born of and practiced in hunger and war.

In all things, these two cubs were combative and competitive, often testing and probing at each other, each with his own internal drive, powerful living drives that forced them at each other time and again. But sometimes the older would drop his voice and speak some instruction, and the younger, without hesitation, would break off battle and they would return to their mother's side. Backs placed against her body, they assumed the role of vigilant sentries, protectors of their protector.

By journey's end, winds of change had filled their lungs. Old-country air had been replaced by new. For my father, the first steps in his new land were on Ellis Island. There he met his own father, wondered at flat-roofed houses, and became America.

Obituary: Blue Fish Special
(1989)

In a previously unheard of display of animus toward animation cuisine, Stuart A. Green of Sharon lured the famous Blue Fish of Dr. Seuss fame from its school and onto his platter and proceeded to devour the little fish, whose career as a child educator had spanned more than a quarter of a century.

Green, no relation to the colored fish in the Seuss book, is said to have formed an alliance with the Red Fish in a cartoon color war over space in the Seuss classic.

Blue Fish's dismembered remains were found in a trash container behind the Legal Seafood restaurant in Chestnut Hill.

Forensic experts on the scene report that Blue Fish was repeatedly stabbed with sharp instruments, probably a knife and a fork.

Denying mob connections, Green responded to police interrogators with a fishy series of burps.

The Carnie Kid rides again

(1994)

Carnivals and circuses have always held a special attraction for me. When I was a kid, I wanted to be The Kid who packed up and ran off with a traveling show. With a carnival in Sharon last week and the big-top soon to arrive, I recall a Fourth of July weekend thirty-five years ago when the carnival came to town and a 12-year-old Sharon kid had a chance to seize his dream.

Doyle Bros. Carnival was hired for the Fourth of July celebration and the carnies set up shop at the Sacred Heart School, now called Deborah Sampson Park. Kids gathered to stare at the clutches, gears, and belts that drove the big machines. They stood in awe as the crew raised the center pole of the Jenny, which is what carnies call the Merry-go-'round.

One thing the carnival boss could count on was that some 12-year-old kid would step out of the crowd and ask to join the show. The crew chief at Doyle Bros. knew how to say 'no' to a kid and have some fun at the same time. One year, his game backfired on him.

"Jelly Bean," Bobby Doyle said to the 12-year-old on the last night of Sharon's carnival. "You come back when it's time to break down and we'll see if you can get a job."

When the fairway lights went out, the crew assembled in front of Bobby Doyle for breakdown assignments and the 12-year-old walked right up to the boss.

"I've told this Jelly Bean here that he can become a carnie if he can prove to us he can do the job," Doyle announced to his crew. "Is that all right with everyone?" The carnies had seen this act before and they were looking forward to what came next. They clapped their hands and agreed that the proposition was fair.

"Okay, Jelly Bean, all you have to do is remove this bolt and you have a job," Bobby Doyle said. He fingered the ends of a nut and bolt that passed through a leg of the Ferris Wheel frame. The carnie boss easily loosened the nut.

Shocked by his great good luck, the 12-year-old stepped forward and touched the bolt. Whack! An electrical charge shot through his body. The kid jumped backwards. The carnies let out a great howl of laughter and applause and yelled encouragement to the kid to try again.

"Jelly Bean, I can not believe you want to be a carnie and can't even loosen off this bolt," said Bobby Doyle in a loud voice and exaggerated cadence. Then, placing his hands on the bolt again, the carnie boss casually loosened more of the thread.

The 12-year-old let cold fury focus his mind. Under no circumstances would he allow himself to release that bolt until the task was done. He stepped forward, his mind set against the shock he knew was coming. He grabbed the nut and bolt. Pain surged through his body. His hands twisted at the nut, and he managed one full turn. Then, muscles twitching, his concentration broke and he jumped back in failure.

The carnies applauded and hooted.

"What do you say, Jelly Bean? We'll give you one last try. If you can't do it this time, you just go on home to your mama, okay? Look here, there's nothing to it. Just loosen off the bolt." As he spoke, Doyle loosened and tightened the nut up and down the bolt threads. The kid studied the carnie boss intently, then nodded and stepped up to the Ferris Wheel leg. The carnies moved in behind him for one last laugh. Bobby Doyle, hands on hips, stood beside the leg, taunting.

Concentrating every ounce of his wiry frame into the motion, the Sharon kid lunged forward and slammed his head hard against the carnie boss's chest. Bobby Doyle fell backward and landed on the ground away from the leg. The kid placed his feet squarely on the piece of wood where Bobby Doyle had been standing during his demonstrations and easily removed the bolt from the Wheel.

The carnies went wild. They howled and hooted, clapped their hands, and slapped the kid on the back. Even Bobby Doyle was laughing from where he lay sprawled on the ground. He reached into his pocket and pulled out a $20 dollar bill. Holding it out to the kid, he laughed. "Here Jelly Bean, you earned it."

But the kid hadn't come for $20; he was there to join the carnival.

Bobby Doyle tried half-heartedly to shake the kid off, but the other carnies weren't having any of that. A deal's a deal after all, and among the carnies, the 12-year-old Sharon kid had won the right to join the crew, fair and square.

That night, the kid worked disassembling the Ferris Wheel and loading its parts into one of the big tractor-trailer trucks. When everything was packed away, he climbed into a truck cab, exhausted, and fell asleep.

When he awoke, the trucks were on the road, moving on, as carnivals do, to the next town and the next set-up.

He spent the morning working with the other members of the Wheel crew. It was only when they were called over to help raise the center pole of the Jenny that Bobby Doyle discovered the kid had made the trip to Brockton.

Around noon, a white Cadillac drove onto the lot and everyone lined up for his pay. The carnie boss called the names and each man was paid in cash. Bobby Doyle called, "Jelly Bean, it's your turn." Old Man Doyle, the paymaster, looked at the kid and asked him how old he was. When he heard he had a 12-year-old working on one of his crews, he took his son, Bobby, aside. They talked for a while, then Old Man Doyle threw back his head and laughed out loud.

Peeling off two $20 bills from his roll, the old man patted the kid on the shoulder, laughed again, and handed him the money. "Bobby will call your parents and get you back to Sharon," Old Man Doyle said and patted the kid once more.

Bobby Doyle made the call. The kid was supposed to have stayed over at a friend's house and hadn't been missed at all. His parents arrived at the lot late in the afternoon. They looked at their son, covered in grease and grime, and went off to talk with Bobby Doyle. And then—like in the kid's greatest dream—they agreed to let him stay on with the carnival through its run in Brockton and Foxboro, with the proviso that he call home every day.

Two years later, when the Jack Frost Carnival was setting up rides at Cobb's Corner, a kid walked up to the carnie boss and asked for a job. The boss told him to beat it, but when the kid said he had worked for Doyle Bros., the carnie asked if he had ever worked on the Jenny.

"Just helped out with the center pole," the kid said. "I'm a Wheel man."

"Heck, if you could work for Doyle, I guess you can work for me," the carnie boss said, and he shook the kid's hand.

And the Sharon kid was The Carnie Kid again.

Rolling with the punches

(1992)

The old house near the center of town had been built on the very-very spot where the Earth curves to form its sphere. Floyd knew it from the moment he was born on the floor of the upstairs dressing room. He and his siblings made allowances for it as they climbed and tumbled over each other to get through the fur of their mother's belly.

On this midsummer's day, Floyd lazed on the green hammock, intently licking his front paws, undaunted by the stream of cusses from the two workmen attempting to hang new awnings on the old house. Rolling onto his back, he continued the sensuous licking mantra which made up the better part of his late morning bathing ritual. The hammock swung gently with the movement of his body. His back muscles rippled with contentment. The workmen struggled and swore.

The sun was warm and comforting on Floyd's belly and face. He rolled his eyes closed and traced the veins of his eyelids against the sun. Struggling on the ladders, rivulets of salty sweat burned the workmen's eyes. Back muscles bulged as they fought to set the awnings in place.

Damned old house. Nothing was going right. Joe stretched to fasten an awning clamp. Suddenly his ladder slipped to the right. He grabbed hold of the gutter, fingers and arms straining to pull himself right.

Floyd heard the scrape and looked over. There was nothing to see. In a single fluid motion, he stretched his four paws to the sun and spread the pads to admire his claws. The hammock gently rolled.

"You okay?" Joe's partner called.

"Damn!"

Joe's partner climbed down from his ladder and looked at the awning. "It's still not straight. Try moving the left down a hair."

"I just moved it up," Joe snapped. "Make up your mind." He climbed down to see for himself. "Damn! I just moved it up. Almost got killed for the trouble, too. I'm for leaving it alone and getting the hell out of here. We're already two damn hours behind. Pack up, we've got other jobs to do."

Floyd heard his litter-mate Fluffy approach.

"B'weerr," she called.

Slowly, Floyd rolled and peered over the edge of the hammock. Fluffy had another field mouse. Floyd watched with some interest as the mouse attempted to run. Fluffy waited until the last possible second to chase down the escapee and flip it into the air.

The workmen's truck roared out of the driveway. Fluffy dropped the mouse and sprang onto the hammock. The mouse made for cover in some thick ivy. Fluffy let it go, but noted the track it took. She was a good hunter and would have no trouble catching it, or another, later in the day. The hammock rolled back and forth under Fluffy's footsteps. Floyd squinted and absorbed the sensuous movement.

The screen door slammed. It was Feeder.

"Honey, call the company. They're not straight, " said Feeder looking up at the awnings.

Floyd watched Fluffy's head cock one way and then the other, mimicking Feeder's attempt to reconcile the irreconcilable.

Floyd yawned and stretched and set the hammock in motion again. Once you learn to adjust to the ups and downs, it can be great living on the very-very spot where the Earth curves.

Stones: earth science vs biology
(1994)

There's war in our town.

The parties clash on this issue: If Earth Science replaces Biology in grade nine, will Sharon's children grow up to be park rangers guiding rafts through the Grand Canyon, or Nobel Laureates hob-nobbing with King Gustav? And, of course, the critical question: What's the pay differential between these two options?

The corollary to these questions will surface at future family dinners in introductions such as, "...and this is my son, David, the doctor. You've heard of him?" vs. "This is my son, David, the rock specialist whose earning potential was nipped in the bud, destroyed in the ninth grade, when Earth Science replaced Biology."

That, I think, concisely summarizes the debate.

As it happens, I am rather an expert on this issue, having taken both Earth Science and Biology in the ninth grade.

Not only did I take Biology-I as a freshman, I also took it in the tenth grade. In fact, I took Biology-I over and over, all through high school. I can even recall my teachers by their Latin names, genus, and phylum.

Parents of potential physicians should be upset if their children are denied Biology-I in grade nine as that leaves them a mere three years more to pass the course.

But, potential doctor's Mom, if it's any solace, you can take it from me: Biology-I is a cruel hoax.

Each year, I was asked to draw what I saw through the lens of my microscope. Each effort was returned with a red 'F' scribbled across the drawing. My teachers claimed I had drawn my own eyelash and not the single-celled parmesan I was supposed to have seen under the scope. There was no parmigiana under the lens. Had it been there, surely I would have smelled it.

For me, biology was a lesson in European cuisine. After four years of cutting up snails and frogs' legs, I felt right at home in the best restaurants of Paris.

At the end of my high school career, I should have received a special doctorate in amphibian medicine. I confess, no frog I ever operated on went on to lead a normal life but, in my defense, the same can be said of some practicing surgeons whose patients start off in much better shape than my formaldehyded charges.

By grade twelve, Biology-I was proving to be the fatal hemorrhage in my matriculatory system. With my biological clock running down toward graduation day, I took what I hoped would be my final Biology-I final exam. Myles Marcus, my friend and Biology teacher, invited me to his home to review the results of my effort.

Nothing short of my graduation from high school rested on an additional two points from that test—one more correct answer. Myles implored me to re-examine my examination and uncover some overlooked answer acceptable for a passing grade.

I took up the papers and perused the column of questions I had completed. As was my practice, I had only responded to those questions I was sure of and left my voids blank.

Scanning the column of check marks was easy. Each question I had answered was correct. I knew about osmosis and enzymes, chromosomes, and small intestines. Nictitating membranes were no strangers to my experience. And then I saw it. A single, red, 'X' beside a question I had answered.

"Define alveoli," it read.

I had responded, "Typing misprint. Letter transposition. Question should read, 'Define ravioli'—Italian cuisine; a pasta stuffed with either meat or cheese, and served with a delicious tomato or meat sauce."

Myles looked at the question. He re-read my answer. Seeing the misprint on the exam, he marked my response correct and added two points to my score, thus pushing me up out of high school and down into life.

Myles went on to head the guidance department at Sharon High School. Although, I never operated on another hopper, I did go on to sample gourmet foods all over the world.

Returning to the war zone, I present an alternative future dinner:

"David, meet Dr. Blah-Blah, who has asked your sister to marry him. Look at the beautiful engagement ring with all the diamonds the Doctor has given her."

David glances at the ring. "They're rhinestones, Ma."

The Doctor gulps. "I'm sorry, Mrs. J. Times are tough. Managed healthcare and all. I didn't know your son was an expert in precious stones."

"Sure he's an expert in stones. And with his own sand-and-gravel business. The biggest on the East Coast, I might add. And all thanks to ninth-grade Earth Science."

David passes the plate of frogs' legs parmesan to his proud mother.

A short campaign
(1994)

I take my hat off to Marjorie, Bill, and Lou, and all people who run for public office, in recognition of the endless hours of hard work and determination that go into placing a candidacy, a record, and one's future into the hands of the people.

Seeking approval is a wrenching ordeal, waiting for the votes to be tallied to learn if you are among the accepted—or rejected. I know. I have some experience in the exhilarating but sometimes cruel world of electoral politics.

It was years ago. Back in the days when Henrietta Becker was a vote-tallier in town. Back in the days of paper ballots and magic markers. Back in the days when a black spot next to a name was a vote of confidence. Quite the opposite of 'tip 'im the black spot' in Treasure Island, these were spots of favor and approval. These were votes.

On the way to the polls, Jody and I entered the 'Free-Fire Zone' in front of the high school, the area populated by the gauntlet of hopefuls and their most ardent supporters, many of whom we knew well and between whom we had to choose. We accepted handouts from partisans and referenda supporters until, at last, we arrived at 'Safety Sidewalk,' that point twenty-five yards in front of the gym doors— past 'One-Last-Chance' for campaigners, and the start of our solitary path to the 'Cubicles of Decision.'

We checked in at our precinct table, received our ballots and black-spotters, and took adjoining booths on the right side of the gym.

As I dotted down my ballot, Jody stuck her head around into my booth. "Who are you voting for for Sheriff?" she asked.

I looked at the ballot. A person unknown to me was running unopposed for the office of Sheriff. My general practice is to skip over the unopposed candidates unless I know them and, in this case, I didn't. Consequently, I'd left the box beside Sheriff unmarked.

Like a flash, it struck me.

Every voting booth comes equipped with a pencil, giving voters the option of writing in Mickey Mouse where appropriate. For example, in a hypothetical contest between George Bush and Michael Dukakis, clearly Mickey Mouse would have appeal. Today, instead of Mickey Mouse, people write in cartoon characters like H. Ross Perot. In one election, after working in New Hampshire to elect Eugene McCarthy, I used one of those Sharon High pencils to write in Bobby Kennedy's name for President. An act that angered most of my friends, but which I consider among the best purposes to which I have ever put a pencil in my life.

Anyway, the thought hit me that I might like the title of 'Sheriff.' I told Jody to write me in and put the black spot next to my name. I wrote my name on the ballot and dotted the box.

As we voted late in the afternoon, I didn't have time to mount the intense campaign I would have run had I decided to be Sheriff earlier in the day. As the polls closed, I knew I was in for an uphill race all the way.

Considering the tension, I was still able to settle down to a night's sleep and await the morning's fateful campaign results.

After a good breakfast, I put in my call to Mrs. Becker. I was pretty sure the news would not be good. When she answered, I asked if I had won the Sheriff's race. She told me I hadn't. Naturally, I was disappointed. "But," I said, "at least I got two votes."

"Two votes? You didn't get two votes. You only got one!"

I put down the phone and looked across the breakfast table at my loving wife, Jody, expecting to find guilt-ridden betrayal written all over her face.

"I thought he would do a better job than you," she said, and she grabbed the last bite of my bagel and popped it into her mouth.

It was a lesson in the democratic process. I had just learned the true meaning of 'ONE MAN—ONE VOTE.'

A town in two acts

(1990)

ACT I: A drizzly day

It's a drizzly Sunday morning. I'm standing alone before the pad-locked gates of the Mountain Street Landfill. (Townies read: I'm down at the dump.) I can't help but think of the history and traditions now locked away behind this chain-link fence. With the town election approaching, I realize I've returned to this place, as I have time and again in years past, to pick through Sharon's political garbage. It was here, at the dump, among the thousands of trashbags and seagulls, that I met my first politicians.

Year after year, candidates and referenda were presented first at the dump. Selectmen, committee members, and townspeople all assembled at the dump for the Sunday morning trashfling/townmeeting. Bad ideas could be hurled over the piles of burning refuse into the gully beyond, never to be seen again. But, as the town grew and its problems grew, the dump began to fill up. Layer heaped upon layer, until the whole political landscape became a solid mound with no chasm left into which our trash could be tossed.

And then they closed the dump forever.

Truck service now removes small items of trash from curbside, but the hazardous waste, the toxic and dumb ideas, the garbage that was once hurled into the chasm, well that stuff piles up in people's attics and cellars, and the pile keeps growing.

ACT II: A drizzly day

It's a drizzly Saturday morning. Tax time again. Happily for me, my accountant now supplies me with pre-addressed, giant, white envelopes clipped to my returns so I can't mail the wrong return to the wrong government. That seems to work out really well. Once, before he started addressing envelopes for me, I had to pay a tax to New York State. I addressed the envelope myself and mailed it off to Albany. About six months later, I received a receipt and thank-you letter written in Albanian.

So, this morning, I went to the post office to mail off my returns. A huge placard-toting crowd had taken over the sidewalk. On the outskirts of the mob, I stopped to talk to a friend. Suddenly, someone slapped me on the back and grabbed a tax return out of my hand. "Hey, hold on there," I shouted. But my return was already being passed from hand to hand to hand throughout the crowd.

I waded in after it. People kept whacking at my back. Each time I was close enough to reach for the envelope, someone grabbed my hand and gave it a hard squeeze. Oh, no, I thought, I must have run into the special anti-fraud unit from the Department of Revenue.

I went to review the return in my mind and realized I hadn't actually read it before I signed it. Hey, that's what accountants are for. So I won't have to read all that line-12-and-subtract stuff. I just sign where the accountant puts the little red checks. I hope he didn't try to write off those cats as dependents again this year. If this mob sees that, it'll trample me into a tiny blot on the sidewalk.

I knew George Keverian was looking right at me in the ad when he pointed his finger and said, "Blah, blah... something-or-other...tax package." I should have listened to my mother. She warned me, "Get a Republican accountant."

Suddenly, the crowd went silent and, like the Red Sea, it parted. A tall, thin, dark-haired woman in a pin-striped suit walked through. She grabbed me. She hugged me. She held me at arms length. Then she kissed both my cheeks.

"Someday, I may call upon you to do me a service," she intoned as she stared into my eyes. "I can count on your vote?" I looked around at the silent, intent, staring crowd and quickly nodded 'yes.' She pinched and patted my cheeks. "I thought that was a nice touch, the cats." She smiled. From out of the throng, the return was delivered into my hands. A path opened and I entered the post office. At the counter, I held out the envelope.

The postman looked at it. "I can't sign now, I'm on duty."

I looked down at my tax return. Under my signature were hundreds of other signatures. They continued down the page and onto the other side.

It felt good to be part of the body politic. I bought a stamp and dropped the whole mess into the mail slot. Hell, I thought proudly, I told the accountant to write off those cats.

EPILOGUE: A brighter tomorrow

I've been thinking that perhaps it's politicians campaigning in front of the post office, with all those wanted posters on the wall, that causes people to distrust government the way they do today. On the other hand, being wanted could be the very thing that attracts people to politics.

Presidential poultry
(1992)

In the wrestle-mania, freak-show, countdown week before the poll doors opened, Bush and Clinton were cliff hanging, dead heat, tooth-and-nail, neck-and-neck, and making me a nervous wreck. I ate Chinese food three times a day just to get to the fortune cookies.

Candidates, news of candidates, commercials for candidates, commentators, pollsters, gurus, and pundits had boggled my mind so that, instead of once a week, I was in daily therapy with a spin doctor to stop my eyes from rolling.

Sure, I knew where my vote was going. I knew how Sharon would vote. And, of course, Massachusetts was firmly behind Clinton. But the uncertainty of the national outcome kept my eyes riveted on the TV, my ears glued to the radio, the house piled with newsprint, and an emergency oxygen mask strapped to my face.

Bob Dylan, who has scribbled a line for every occasion, wrote, "You don't need a weather man to know which way the wind blows." I went outside and checked the leaves lying dead on my lawn. No help there. If, in fact, the answer was 'blowing in the wind,' how could I get a read on it?

I needed someone who could hit the nail on the head, I called carpenter, Larry VanLeer. Within hours, Larry had attached a Rooster weathervane to the top of my house. As the song goes, "When the rooster crows at the break of dawn...."

In the frosty break of dawn, I stood out on the lawn, looking not toward the heavens for a sign, but to Dylan, the rooster on the roof, to point the way.

Jody and I worked out the signals: If Dylan pointed east toward the rising sun and the new dawn, Clinton would win the election; if Dylan pointed west toward the Pacific and the direction of fleeing American jobs, Bush would win; southwest, Perot. Any other direction, and the election would be thrown into the House of Representatives.

All day Sunday, winds buffeted the rooftop. Dylan didn't move at all. I climbed the ridge pole to have a look. Dylan was stuck. He needed grease. I slapped a big glob of chicken fat under his arrow and waited for it to trickle down his perch. In the cold air, the grease blobbed and I had to shmear it with my finger. Dylan started to move, first one way, then another, vacillating back and forth—Bush, Clinton, Bush, Clinton. I could be inside, warm and watching CNN for all the help I was getting from this dumb cluck.

Monday, midnight, election eve. I lay in bed, heart thumping. High anxiety tensed every synapse. Than I heard a whirring sound. Whoosh, whoosh. The walls of the house shook, the bed rolled. Whoosh!

It was Dylan on the roof.

I jumped out of bed and ran outside to the driveway. Up on the roof, Dylan spun 'round and 'round, head thrown back, nostrils flaring, like a hound on a scent. "Come on, Dylan!" I yelled, jumping up and down in my underwear in the middle of the driveway. "Come on!"

Dylan pointed north and stopped, then due east and stopped again. Then he flipped west and stopped there. Jody rushed out of the house, tying on her robe. "What did he say?" she gasped.

"Rotten chicken. He's not saying anything. First, no winner. Then Clinton. Then Bush. Get me my shotgun. I'll make this bird a lame duck right now!"

Before I could load up, Jody grabbed my arm. "Wait, maybe it's code?"

"What code?"

"Look, he's spelling out a message. N-E-W. New! I think he's saying 'New.' We'll have a new president."

The words were barely out of her mouth when Dylan started to spin; around and around, faster and faster, like the blades of a helicopter at full tilt. The house groaned, and strained, and pulled against its foundation. "Watch out!" I yelled and pushed Jody to the ground. A blood-curdling cock-a-doodle-doo pierced the night. Up and down North Main Street, lights went dark then banged on again, brighter than I had ever seen them before. And all the lights on Main Street were shining on Dylan. And Dylan pointed due east. Clinton would win the election!

Arm in arm, Jody and I climbed the stairs to the house. We started singing another Bob Dylan line. "May you have a strong foundation when the winds of changes shift."

It was a warm feeling, singing the old Dylan songs and knowing the times really were a-changing, even if a hard rain was starting to fall and I was freezing my buns off outdoors in my Fruit of the Looms.

Republicans head out
(1990)

Over the years, Sharon has been lucky to draw folks who settle here as careers dictate a move to the Boston area. In their search to find a nice place to live and to raise a family, they discover Sharon.

Some of these people later look back to roots and families located in distant 'back-homes' and find that their children deserve a chance to get to know aging grandparents and reconnect with family ties.

It can be sad when people leave Sharon to pursue their lives elsewhere, even for the most compelling reasons, sad for them and sad for the friends they have made here. This week, Sharon is losing the Dumler family and, in them, half of Sharon's registered Republicans will be leaving town.

Doug and Cathy Dumler came here from that empty space between New England and California usually referred to as Indian Territory or the Great Plains. It's a land of endless sky and endless wheat fields where people endlessly wear overalls, eat endless stacks of hot cakes, and drink endless gallons of milk from endless metal containers. Out there, the days are spent endlessly dodging tornadoes and rolling oats between palms while endlessly sniffing the chaff for something. Lassie, Billy, and Gramps live out there. And they don't eat margarine.

In that country, all mothers are named 'Mom.' It's a land where people eat Christmas ham and believe in a newer of the 'old time' religions. The inhabitants are modest, frugal people, who waste not and want not. Their economical lifestyle dictates that the hides of the animals they eat must not go to waste, so football is their sport.

Economy is found even in their sparse speech and rare discourse or debate—that's why they vote Republican. They also grow the biggest damned people you ever saw, and Doug and Cathy Dumler are no exceptions.

Doug and Cathy came east to the real America following a bouncing ball. As a New England Patriot family, they found Sharon a very different place from the world they left behind in the land in between paved roads. Being open-minded people, they were all for giving Sharon a go.

When not practicing football or having his bones crunched in a game, Doug, with Cathy at the wheel, would push his early-1950s Buick up and down the streets of Sharon. They never did find a gas pump, but they always knew that when Doug's football career came to an end, they could find work as the tow-truck couple at any local garage.

For a while, the Dumlers joined the Minnesota Vikings, but they kept their home in Sharon and the friendships they built here. Doug returned to the Patriots and went on to get a law degree in order to read the label on the snake oil Billy Sullivan was selling over at Schaefer, Sullivan, and Foxboro stadiums.

Sharon made quite an impression on Cathy. When I first met her, she was already telling risqué gorilla jokes over spicy Mexican food—jokes she certainly didn't learn down at the Grange Hall socials.

Doug formed and joined the Republican Town Committee and soon became its leader and entire membership, running unopposed and being elected chairman on only the second ballot.

While in Sharon, Doug and Cathy had two daughters. I don't know Julie Dumler very well—Jody tells me she is a wonderful child. Ten-year-old Abbie has been my son's loved friend since birth. Zev, Abbie, and Allison Strumski formed a triumvirate from the earliest days of playgroup. Zev lets them practice women's liberation techniques on him. And if either of them go on to become President, much of the credit should go to him. It is a dynamic trio now scattered to the winds. Finding roots can be an uprooting experience.

Doug and Cathy, I know your real reason for moving 'out there' is you are becoming too old to push that Buick up and down the streets of Sharon and—as everyone knows—once you get to Colorado, it's all downhill from there. Good luck from your friends in civilization.

When sparks flew
(1989)

It's appropriate that Family Week ended with the warmth, light, and sparks of a bonfire. After all, aren't those the very characteristics found in families?

Last night, Jody, Zev, and I went to Memorial Beach for the Family Week closing ceremony. With us was Federica, our 19-year-old cousin from Italy, who is staying in Sharon and attending Northeastern University.

I've never known very much about the Italian part of me. We sat on the beach by the flickering firelight and talked about our family, about our grandmother, now dead, who I'd never met and who Federica visited nearly every day of her life. Federica and I—an Italian and an American—first cousins, exploring all that we have in common and the differences a single generation's separation makes in a family.

As we walked from the beach to Big Mama's house on Ames Court, I watched the sparks from the bonfire fly overhead. They reminded me of the first time I'd met cousins from Italy. Sparks flew that day, too.

I was twelve. The family sat down to one of Mama Fisher's famous meals. Seated at the dining room table with us were two 25-years-old cousins just arrived from Italy. They didn't speak any English. An incomprehensible wall of words separated them from me. Once in a while, my mother would translate something, then jump back into Italian, and the cadence would speed up. Italian is spoken at twice the speed of English and I couldn't tell where one word began and another left off.

It didn't really matter. At that moment, my mind was preoccupied with another foreign language—Hebrew.

The phone rang. It was for my father. He went to the kitchen to take the call. From where I sat, I saw the color drain from his face. His fair skin went translucent, then white, then to bright red. He put down the phone and moved into the dining room toward me.

I slipped out of my chair and moved in the opposite direction. Like watching two shapes reflected in a mirror, I synchronized my movements to his and kept the table between us. There, like dancers around a fire, we circled. The Italian din hushed, then went quiet.

Bewildered faces watched the dance circle this way, then that. Silence filled the air like the table filled the space between us. The cousins looked to my mother for explanation, but this even she couldn't translate for them. The language my father was speaking could be understood only in the silent, growing anger of his bright-red face.

My father and I knew that the caller on the phone was Moshe Avital, principal of Temple Israel's Hebrew School, and he had just informed my father that I was expelled.

He wasn't going to catch me. My father and I both realized at the same moment that I could keep that dining room table between us forever. I laughed at the thought—a terrible mistake. Big Daddy backed into the living room and with one lift-and-jerk, he pulled the television off its stand, ripping the plug out of the wall. In the next second, he launched the TV over the table to my right. It hit the wall and fell to the floor with a crash. I stood dead in my tracks and watched it fly, but before I realized the diversion, he was already around the table with a firm grip on my left arm and ear.

As we headed off for the bathroom, I saw the wide eyes of my Italian cousins. Welcome to America. They spoke quietly now, and very, very slowly, so that even I, en route, could make out where the words began and ended. At once, I understood Italian perfectly. Hebrew was going to be a harder instruction. I was going to receive a private lesson and, for a few days, I would have to study standing up in the tradition of the great Hebrew academies of Eastern Europe.

As Federica and I got farther away from the lake, I looked back at the bonfire. I loved the light, the warmth, and the sparks. What a terrific way to end Family Week. Truth be told, from a distance, looking back, I guess I've always loved the sparks best, both at bonfires and in the family. It's the sparks that can fly and start new fires everywhere. How like a family.

Saints and saucers fly

(1990)

Big Mama was born in Italy and lived in that country for the first thirteen years of her life. Having a mama born in a far-away place meant that I got to hear tales of a life far different from my own experiences and from the world I saw around me. Having no picture in my head to relate her stories to, I was forced to create my own images and super- · impose them on the stories Big Mama told.

Mama said that as a child, she was often hungry and hardly ate meat at all. Once-in-a-while, she got to taste pigeon that was raised in nests in the stone walls where she lived. I don't know if they were pigeons or squab because Big Mama spoke Italian back then and pigeon and squab are English words. Mama said that even the tiniest morsel of pigeon was a great treat in her diet—but then, she's never served any for us.

When the steeple on the First Baptist Church Uptown was being painted, I thought of climbing a ladder and bagging Big Mama a feast full of squabs, but somehow I never got around to it. Then the ladders were gone.

I have to admit, I've eaten that type of bird at Chinese wedding banquets. Some Chinese people call it squab, and some say pigeon. It's not at all like shark fin soup, where everyone agrees and calls it shark fin soup.

Many Chinese believe that shark fin soup is an aphrodisiac, but it's always the first course served at an 11-course Chinese wedding banquet, followed by endless rounds of toasts and speeches, the rest of the banquet, and the long drive home from Boston to Sharon. So much time has elapsed from soup to bed that I certainly couldn't swear to its effects.

Chinese tradition says it's good luck for the marriage to serve that soup first, but to my way of thinking, it would be better luck to serve it just before the guests are on the way out the door, or better yet, give it as a party favor in take-out containers.

Anyway, having a mother born in Italy is a special circumstance, and especially if she comes from Assisi.

Everyone in Assisi is related to me, except for the tourists who come in droves to see the shrines to Saint Francis.

When you have a saint in the family, you bear a special burden of responsibility and expect to be held to a higher standard. I know I feel that way and always cook my linguine al dente to commemorate the life of denial that Cousin Frank chose for himself in the mountains overlooking our ancestral home.

And then there's the letter 'H.' There's no sound for it in the Italian language. One of our neighbors on Marie Avenue was Hal Rosenthal. I remember Big Mama saying, "Your brother is at 'al's, go and tell 'im to come 'ome." Sometimes she would say to me, "You, get the 'ell out of 'ere!"

It's been my experience that having a mama from Italy is a life's lesson in demonstrative communication. For example, it would have been uncommon to receive an order unpunctuated by a shoe, plate, or rolling pin flying in my direction. I learned about spatial relationships by calculating the duck-time between the distance, speed, and trajectory of a moving plate and my head. When I first saw Einstein's $E=MC^2$, I screamed, "Eureka! That boy has written the perfect Italian equation." I could never understand why stories about flying saucers were categorized as science fiction. They were real enough at our house.

The first thing my sister, Paula, did when she moved her residence from afloat on a boat in the Atlantic Ocean to terra firma Mansfield, Mass., was to buy goats. That's a really Italian thing to do, and I was jealous as 'ell from the first moment I laid eyes on Chainsaw and Lawn Mower, two black-and-white Nubian goats with soft, floppy ears. When I looked into their big brown eyes, they called to me, "Pa, Paaa." I knew right then and there that their ancestors and mine had met somewhere back in time in the mountains overlooking our Assisi.

With Family Week coming, it's nice to think of where you come from. We Fisher kids are descended from a saint—Francis of Assisi. I think it shows.

New years, old stories
(1992)

I was only a small boy, certainly no more than four or five, when the man came to my grandmother's house.

He sat with her at the kitchen table and spoke in a language that I understood, but couldn't speak. He spoke the language in an unfamiliar way, sometimes using words that even my grandmother needed explained. They spoke in hushed tones, the type adults use to pass secrets, and I hid in the pantry to listen to the story he told.

The man was my grandmother's brother, youngest of thirteen brothers and sisters. My grandmother had been second oldest and the oldest girl. Almost a quarter of a century separated them in age and it wasn't clear to me if my grandmother had even been in Europe when this last brother was born.

They were going over names. Sisters and brothers, their husbands, wives, children, cousins, and what they knew of the fate of each of them.

I heard my grandmother tell of helping her mother with the birth of a sister and how she had been first to hold the newborn. Her brother said a few quiet words. Then he reached across the table and took my grandmother's hand. Her body shuddered. She broke into sobs.

I stepped out from my hiding place and started toward her. She saw me and quickly tried to compose herself. Her voice was hoarse as she told me to go out and play. She pressed a sugar cube into my hand and softly stroked my cheek. I went to the porch and lay on the sofa under the kitchen window and stuffed the sugar cube into my mouth, rolling the sweetness around with my tongue.

My uncle continued. It was like a far away, once-upon-a-time tale, only my grandmother knew the characters' names and could tell the beginning of their story. Her youngest brother told the endings and they were always the same—murdered.

More than forty years have past. Rosh Hashanah, the Jewish New Year, has arrived. I prepare a slice of apple dipped in honey and put it in my mouth. "For a sweet year," I declare. I taste the sweetness rolling over my tongue. The news is on the radio, a story from Somalia or Bosnia. The sweetness of honey is in my mouth.

I was a small boy listening under my grandmother's window with a piece of sugar in my mouth. My granduncle told a once-upon-a-time tale in hushed tones. I didn't like the story. In the end everyone died. Why tell a story like that? Even my grandmother cried. Why have a story where everyone is murdered in the end?

Soul music
(1990)

In a few days, Harold Lew will retire as cantor of Temple Israel. For many of us who grew up in and with the Temple, Cantor Lew's retirement will mark the end of an era distinguished by the strength, constancy, and welcoming warmth of our cantor's song.

I'm not sure if communities choose cantors who represent the congregation's view of itself, or if the cantor shapes the congregation. Perhaps it's a synthesis of the two. I've been to synagogues where I've heard operatic cantors—performers—voiced pitch-perfect in clarion announcement to the heavens. Each of them has made me appreciate the special 'Everyman' quality in Cantor Lew's voice all the more.

By the word 'Everyman,' one should not infer pedestrian or ordinary—quite the opposite. His is a special blend of harmonic sounds encompassing notes ranging above the congregation, then dropping and broadening to a soft melodic hum—the sound itself almost the prayer—that unique sound that makes Cantor Lew's voice so special, so accessible. His voice is like a great prayer shawl enveloping the Temple Israel family.

The position of cantor (*hazan* in Hebrew) is the unifying singing voice for the congregation. While each congregant's voice is individual, when blended together, they become the people's song. The hazan harnesses the collective whole, leads the traditional tune, and encourages the harmonies. Over the past 35 years, Harold Lew's has been the collective voice of Temple Israel and I have found it resonant of my innermost voice, as well. His tones have carried my tune and voiced my song.

I was one of the few students to become Bar Mitzvah at Temple Israel without having been trained by Cantor Lew.

The date had been set for my Bar Mitzvah—Dec. 5, 1959. That summer, my father placed me under the tutelage of Mr. Bass, the sexton of what was then the two-room Temple Israel. Ordinarily, six months is plenty of time to learn Bar Mitzvah readings backward and forward, but I was leaving for New York Military Academy come September and wouldn't have any lessons from September through the December date.

Working with me through the summer must have been a trying time for the old sexton. I know it was for me. We studied the musical notations and the words and finally put the two together.

From the start of school in September, I returned home only once—for Thanksgiving weekend. That Saturday, I went to Temple Israel and watched another boy become Bar Mitzvah. That was my last chance to see one before my own.

New York Military Academy was not a hotbed of Jewish culture. In fact, as I recall, in that respect, it was a very long way from Sharon.

On Friday, Dec. 4, I boarded a bus from Cornwall-on-the-Hudson to New York City and caught my flight to Boston. When I awoke the next morning, I put on my best suit—my only suit—a navy-blue dress uniform with 48 gold buttons and tuxedo-like tails, and a single piece of cross webbing with a gold breast plate, red sash, and white gloves. When I entered the Temple, my father gave me a new prayer shawl.

At the appropriate point in the service, Cantor Lew nodded for me to take my place on the bimah. When I was called to read, I did what Jewish boys have done for centuries. The text easily rolled out in the ancient melodies. My speech was made and it contained the first hint of my realization of a world less hospitable to Jews.

Standing there next to Cantor Lew was, perhaps, his only non-pupil, dressed unlike any other in the Temple's history, already in transition as he formally took his place among his people.

Because he wasn't my teacher, the teacher who got me to my Bar Mitzvah day, I can step back and admire and wonder at the vast number of students Cantor Lew did prepare, and at the quality of teaching he's done. He taught my daughter, Tamara, and it never occurred to me that he would not be the one to teach my son, Zev. Such is the institution he has become at Temple Israel.

As a small boy in the synagogue during Friday evening Shabbat services, I would close my eyes as Mrs. Feldman played chords on the organ behind the Cantor's voice. The melding of those two beautiful instruments into one sound is one of the most enduring and peaceful memories I have carried with me all my life. It is what prayer sounds like in my soul.

During Yom Kippur's Kol Nidre prayer, I have felt the flush of my skin as Cantor Lew's voice blended and focused the voices and thoughts of hundreds of people, leading and joining them, almost trance-like, in the ascent to a higher spiritual plane.

Although he is retiring, I believe that whenever I hear or think about the chants of my people, I will hear them broadened into the distinctive sounds of Cantor Lew's tones. For the past 35 years, his has been the voice to the resonant tune in me and the harmony to my song.

New guys
(1994)

Black clouds hung in the sky. The New Guys, dressed in fatigues and ponchos, were formed into two platoons and marched down Faculty Road past where the pavement ended, toward the small, concrete underpass that ran beneath the highway and led to hundreds of wooded acres known as 'the Farm.'

The Maj. marched at the head of the formation and Lt. Winters called the cadence from the left side. Maj. began whistling *Bridge Over the River Kwai*. We picked it up. The formation stepped out nicely, striding in time with the music.

A quarter of a mile before the underpass stood a small grove of trees. Set among the trees were a squalid shack and filthy chrome trailer where the school's two trash men lived. They were known to us as 'Sock' and 'Stench,' and, as far as we knew, they had no other names. As we marched past their grove, a blast of wind pushed against our formation. The trash truck was nowhere to be seen.

Winters, a senior, had recently been transferred from 'C' company where he was a private for the previous two years. Then one day he appeared as a lieutenant in our company of middle-school cadets.

All cadet officers were high school juniors or seniors. And, although middle school students could be non-commissioned officers—corporals and all variety of sergeants—we were New Guys, first year cadets, and as such, not eligible for any rank at all. We were 'the scum of the earth' and were often called upon to say so by any cadet who had attained the status of 'Old Guy'—anyone who was at least a second-year cadet.

Maj. was a Tactical Officer, an adult and mentor to our middle school company. He wore the uniform of a United States Army Major.

Some Tac officers were on assignment from the army as ROTC instructors, others were Army retired, still others held school-designated rank, which may have been honorary or State Guard. With the exception of the Maj., we didn't differentiate between them.

The weather worsened. Wind whipped at our ponchos and made our platoons appear like ghostly rectangles eerily moving through twilight. We pushed ahead. Sheets of rain raked the other side of the highway. The newly 'made' Lt. Winters let on he didn't like New Guy duty. We knew we wouldn't like him either. This was our first trip with him to the Farm. A raw afternoon slosh through cold muck was certain to bond us together forever with good feeling. Clouds sucked away the daylight. Early afternoon was already darker than dusk. One glance across the highway foretold a bleak afternoon.

Winters, head high, called cadence from the left side of first platoon. The sky barked out a sharp clap of thunder. As if in response to an order, I side-stepped to the right of the formation, marked time, and dropped back in the column until I marched beside the Spaz and Jonny Hawkins.

The song ended and Winters spun to the rear, calling out a half-step and cadence response. We all shouted back with the count, covering 32 marching beats. He spun again and worked his way forward. Head tossed back, he looked like the owner of a new, red Corvette convertible putting it through its paces. I was ready to put the top up and head for the garage.

We arrived at the underpass. The platoons closed ranks to fit through. The Maj. started singing *Charley Brown*. The sound echoed off the concrete. Hawk, Spaz, and I cut out to the right. The formation passed on through to the Farm. From behind the embankment, we watched it disappear into darkness, then we headed for the grove near the shacks.

We stacked our rifles near a fallen tree and Hawk lit us up three Marlboros in his mouth at one time with his Zippo, using the two-finger-and-thumb technique he was the unquestioned master of, him being from Brooklyn and having a substantial head start with Zippos over the Spaz and me.

We lay against the tree and sucked the smoke deep into our lungs. I snapped my jaw and formed a perfectly-shaped smoke 'O.' I followed the white circle as it rose and broadened and headed toward the sky. Over our grove, sheaves of sun streamers broke through the clouds.

It was going to be a great day after all.

Tracks

(1990)

The railroad comes through our town: the Amtraks that whiz by, the rare freight that chugs along, and the bedroom-town commuter trains that stop at our station to take the town to work and bring it home again. And for as long as trains have passed through Sharon, children have been drawn to the tracks to watch and wander, wonder and wave. It was like that for me when I first walked the tracks as a nine-year-old. Walking the once familiar route now with my nine-year-old son, Zev, drew me back and made me smile on an idle afternoon like so many I had spent along that cinder path.

It was Murray Armstrong who first showed me the entrance to that wondrous system of woods, swamps, brooks, and paths that surround the Industrial Revolution's most enduring swath through town.

Murray asked me if I would bring a hatchet and help build something in the woods behind Pleasant Park Road. We crossed South Main Street and started along a trail that led into the woods. Soon we branched off down a slope and came to a tree-canopied clearing.

A brook ran through the clearing. On the other side, a group of kids with hatchets and axes were building a log cabin. Amazing in its construction, worlds apart from the three-story, board tree house I was building and remodeling in my back yard, this was a notched-log, real log cabin. Its walls were already taller than I was and it was being built by kids only a few years older than me.

The scene could have included Hawkeye and Chingachgook stopping by the brook for a drink of water and it wouldn't have surprised me any more than the image of boys notching and fitting in front of me.

In an instant, I was addicted to the scene and the place. But early in this memory, before the cabin was finished and while we were away, someone knocked it down and dumped the logs into the nearby swamp.

No one ever made an effort to build it again, but the memory of the cabin, the brook, and the clearing remain with me to this day in mixed colors of pine, fern, and swampy greens, of dark humus soil layered over in rust-gold pine needles, as diffused light filters through the leaf canopy.

From the clearing, a path led to the railroad tracks. But along the way, there were oak-treed hills to climb, wild blueberries to pick, and a massive dead tree to sit beside. As I sat and silently ate my berries, I'd watch birds fly in and out of their nests, squirrels build up their winter stocks, and woodpeckers tap Morse on the dead tree's bark. And there, a few yards away, touching all that diversity of life, sound, and stillness—the rail.

Suddenly, the piercing wail of a horn in the distance.

An engineer, either at the Garden Street underpass or the railroad station, warned of an approaching train.

The horn was the 'get ready' signal. In the woods, living motion detectors went to alert—the squirrel's upright stance, darting eyes, twitching ears said something incredible was about to happen.

At the sound, I scrambled to the embankment always arriving in time to see what treasure was being offered up: a giant, speeding locomotive—tons of steel spewing black smoke to the sky, hurling firebolts from its undercarriage, light and detail literally streaking past, a come-and-gone sight with a single sound blast, first peaking, then screaming, then gone to silence; or the other thing—a freight train, rhythmically clanking at each tie-joint, slow enough to allow me to register every wheel and rivet, every stenciled faraway place. And, if I was lucky, there was time to place my penny on the track and have it elongated into railroad art to be retrieved after the caboose passed and the trainman waved his hand at me.

Zev and I walk beside the track. I'm bemused, transfixed, as I watch his sneakers scuff the ground, drag-drawing half circles in the cinder bed, scribed there by 90-odd pounds of life, to remain until natural erasers scrub them away. Beside us, hundreds ride steel-on-steel along the same track and leave no scratch or trace that lasts as long as one small boy's dragging sneaker mark.

For my nine-year-old, like his father before him, each yard along the track yields new treasures in iron spikes and train debris. Looking down the parallel lines to the horizon, my son repeats a story he learned in school of the golden spike driven at the joining of track, East and West.

Touching the track bed are embankments to climb, woods to survey, brooks to follow. I had wanted to show my son an old network of paths but, like with the log cabin, a stranger came while I was away. With a match, an unknown changed the woods and paths forever—fixing them, for me, forever as they once were.

I guess in towns like Sharon, where the Amtraks pass and the commuter trains stop, kids will always discover the tracks and love what they find there.

The school that teaches from memory

(1990)

Halls that once echoed the sounds of laughter and slamming locker doors are silent now save for the quiet, occasional sounds of flaking paint and falling plaster. Walking the empty corridors and classrooms of the Wilber School that had served Sharon as High School, Intermediate, Middle, and Junior High was, for me, a journey back in time.

Memories accompanied me through the desolation. Once, long ago, as a seventh grader, it would have been unthinkable for me to have these rooms to myself, to touch and explore away from the watchful eyes of teachers.

Here was Mort Kaufman's science lab. I fingered the gas fittings that once fired Bunsen burners and remembered blowing heated tubes into glass baubles. Shelves, now empty and askew, once held an array of test tubes, beakers, and ring stands that could be fitted together to distill water or simply to challenge the presumption of alkalinity through the use of a litmus test.

I passed through the tiny A.V. room and into Miss Fleming's lab, then downstairs to Miss Burns' social studies classroom where I had learned the names of places like Guatemala and Honduras and that the main export of Colombia was coffee. That year, Senator John F. Kennedy was running for re-election and Miss Burns split the class in half, naming some of us Kennedy supporters and assigning the others to his Republican opponent, Vincent J. Celest. One of the Segal twins volunteered to be spokesperson for the Republican.

I stood in the doorway of Mrs. Baker's homeroom class and remembered the morning our perfectly-coifed, white-haired teacher read the lunch menu followed by the Twenty-third Psalm. Someone whispered. Mrs. Baker looked up from her Bible. A discernible spasm rippled over her face. The class went still. The seventh grader in my seat quivered. Mrs. Baker—model of nurturing, placid grandmotherliness—contorted, transformed, and exploded in wrathful indignation. A fireball shot from her mouth toward the transgressor. I saw it fly. Then I heard the 'click.' In their fervor to bite off a seventh-grade head, Mrs. Baker's dentures hurled themselves right out of her mouth. But without the rest of her body to accompany them, the chompers had dropped harmlessly to the floor.

Stooping to pick up her teeth, the 'alien' Mrs. Baker broke the spellbinding glare that held us terrorized and, in doing so, was instantly restored to a sweet, grandmotherly figure right before our eyes. She handed the Bible to one of my wide-eyed classmates and told her to continue with the Psalm. The bell rang and we filed out to class, our soft-spoken homeroom mother standing at the door.

The year 1959: pretty Jody MacPhail and her ethereal friend, Leslie Chase, took the train to Boston and Filene's Basement to buy dresses for the seventh-grade dance, 'Sea Cruise.' Dance night found the gym-cafeteria draped in fishnet, with sea horses and other creatures-la-mer forming a seascape canopy as the eighth-grade 'Shytones' (Lee Urrows, Bernie Cunningham, Donnie Whedon, and Bob Cawley) sang their first gig.

The boy's locker room opened into the gym. Today it's a storeroom for an assortment of out-of-date books and discarded junk. But some of the original metal lockers remain as they were thirty or more years ago.

Gym class was over. Bobby G. and I were the last two left in the locker room. Opening his gym bag, Bobby produced a 3-inch long, barber-pole-striped firecracker, packed hard like a stick of dynamite. I produced a match. The fuse shot to life, spewing like a sparkler. The locker slammed shut and Bobby and I dove through the gym door. The clean, sharp, ear-piercing explosion sounded, then amplified and echoed through the metal lockers and tiled room. The shock wave chased us into the gym and rippled and pealed throughout the building. What a sound. What an incredible sound! Nothing compared to it until I heard anti-aircraft fire almost ten years later.

I remember being led past Mrs. Hardy, the school secretary, sitting at her desk. I remember the tick of the long-pendulum clock as we entered the principal's office to see Mr. Koskella and receive our three-week suspensions.

How could we have done it? The answer remains as much a mystery to me today as it was back then. But, then, how could we not? The details of the punishment are long forgotten, but the memory of that sound still echoes in my ears.

All seventh-grade boys wanted Miss Prendergast for math. She was a shining light in our long day. We wanted to watch her write equations on the blackboard. We wanted to watch her assign homework. We wanted to watch her do anything, even if it was math. Walking through her classroom all these years later, I remember that we learned something more than equations in that math class.

I walked into the auditorium. Sunlight streamed through the windows and highlighted the pastel greens of the stage curtain and walls exactly as I knew them. Even the effects of grime and neglect couldn't diminish the architectural beauty of the room with its low-slung balcony and hanging, glass chandeliers. I was assailed by memories. I stood in the very spot where, as a small boy and years before I was old enough to attend the Wilber School, I stood with my father and signed up to play in Little League baseball for the first time. It was in this room that, as junior high students, we watched movies once a month. Movies like *Mr. Smith Goes to Washington*. But *Mr. Smith* was not the only civics lesson I remember from that auditorium.

I remember the night Walter Cronkite came to a meeting there. I was too young to get in, but a policeman let me sneak through the overflow crowd and watch from a back corner as Sharon wrestled with itself, its history, change, and the United States Constitution to determine how the town would separate church and state in its schools. That was the Great Christmas Tree Debate.

Some of the words and sentiments spoken that night between people standing near me echo and reverberate in my ear and throughout my life far louder than the sound of the firecracker in the locker room. They contain no memory of joyous mischief, only the sadness that carnage and war bring.

The doors to the Wilber School are locked now. I've finished browsing. I walk across the lawn and turn to take it all in. The architecture, balconies, and frescoes are amazing, perhaps even beautiful. A building from another era.

The old school's service to the town is ended. It was a school for and from a different time. It remains to teach its best lessons now through our memories.

Dead to rights

(1992)

There is a tale teachers tell. The Angel of Death arrived at a classroom and gently tapped the teacher on the shoulder. "It's time to go," the Angel whispered softly.

"Shove off, Turkey," the teacher replied, hands planted on hips. "I'm not going anywhere. Didn't they tell you? I have tenure. Take it up with my Union!"

The Angel went to the Teachers' Union and a long negotiation ensued. Neither side would give an inch. The Angel tried to explain that he had the responsibility for keeping order in the world, that death is something that comes to all people. It was well known that the teacher hadn't been well for quite some time and had not been able to conduct proper classes for many years.

The Union listened attentively and even agreed that the Angel's mission was important and necessary for mankind and for the students, too, but that having been said, it still refused to break solidarity and remove the teacher from the classroom for any reason not explicitly covered in the Contract.

So the Angel of Death returned to the classroom and removed life from the teacher's body. And when the building administrators tried to have the corpse removed from the classroom, the Union filed a grievance with the National Labor Relations Board and set up a picket line outside the classroom door.

Parents asked that their children be provided with a live teacher, but the principal explained that there were only two classrooms allocated for that grade and the one with the live teacher was already filled to the maximum capacity permitted under the terms of the Contract.

As for the children in the dead teacher's class, they weren't upset at all as the teacher's performance hadn't changed noticeably after death. They still went to lunch and recess when the bells rang and left for the lavatory when the need arose.

When the teacher died, the classroom television was on and it remained on. Sometimes the children would get rowdy and one of the Union picketers would poke his head in the door and ask them to quiet down. The children settled back, watched television, and waited for the bells to ring.

Some of the other teachers were anxious and upset about having a dead teacher in the building. Teachers who complained to the Union leadership were branded traitors and stooges. Solidarity forever meant exactly that—forever. After all, just because the teacher was dead didn't mean there weren't a few worse 'live' teachers in classrooms. If the Union gave in on the 'dead'-dead teacher issue, the school committee might want to remove some 'live'-dead teachers and the whole tenure system would become a joke.

The school began to smell.

An emergency meeting of the school committee, superintendent, assistant superintendent, parents, and Teachers' Union representatives was called. The Angel of Death was asked to attend. The agenda was simple—how to effectuate the removal of a rotting, tenured teacher from the classroom.

For 40 days and 40 nights, they pondered. No one said a word. From time to time, the Angel had to leave to make a business call. Finally, on the stroke of midnight on the fortieth night, the Angel spoke.

"Friends," he began, "and we are all friends here," she continued (an angel can change gender at will.). "Why don't we join our philosophies?"

"Where I come from, we have a saying, 'Raise the dead.' And when you have a marginal student, you say, 'When in doubt, promote it out.' Why not give the dead teacher a raise and a promotion, bury the body in a closet down wind with an important sounding title on the door, and shut off that damn TV set?"

All present saw the wisdom of this plan.

So it was written and so it was done.

That same night, in the place where angels meet, they were also evaluating. The Head Angel spoke. "That was a stupid business with the teacher in the classroom. Never zap a teacher in the classroom—it's the first rule of common sense.

"We've been discussing your performance and, except for that saving bit there at the end, you have become a disaster as an Angel of Death. We have decided to relieve you of your duties and let you go. We're sorry, but we feel it's for the good of all dying things."

The Angel of Death put his wings on his hips. "I'm sorry you feel that way. Perhaps you have forgotten. I still have friends in high places. Let me remind you that I'm a tenured Angel of Death and my union dues are up to date. I can be a disaster twice over and you will never remove me from my post."

The other angels went into executive session and, after a short while, asked the Angel of Death to join them. "Could we offer you a bonus, incentive raise, and a desk job?"

"Now you're talking." The Angel rubbed his wings together. "Solidarity forever!"

It never rains but it pours
(1993)

"The category is Pot Pourree. For $1000, 'My grass is dead and I don't care.' Take it, Herb."

"What is a catchy song title?"

"Wrong. Socrates?"

"What is Truth?"

"Right."

I love *Jeopardy*, don't you? I love *Jeopardy* almost as much as I hate my lawn. Every year, that green growing patch of artificial nature needs nurturing. Rake, mow, kill dandelions before Big Mama eats them, lime, fertilize, water, mow, water, mow, rake.

It's like having an alien squatter stake out 40,000 square feet around my house and demand goods and services.

This year, it's dead and I'm free. Free not to mow. Free not to buy a new lawn mower. Free to spend my money on movies, candle-lit restaurants, and red licorice. Free of Eau de Ben Gay. Free to sit on the porch, like Jody, with a newspaper in my lap, or free to survey my brown holdings, strumming Woody Guthrie dust-bowl ballads on my gee-tar. Free even to write a song called *My Grass is Dead and I Don't Care.*

The other morning while I exultantly strode my powdery, brown earth, sun-sapped rivulets of salty perspiration poured from my body, providing the only precipitation I would permit to reach that crunchy thatch.

A funnel-shaped column of dust whirled around me. Hot winds whipped my white-terry robe. From inside the column, the strains of music. The music rose, built, crescendoed, and ricocheted from each swirling, dust particle. I threw my arms wide to the heavens. My robe billowed. The music swelled. It was the theme from *Lawrence of Arabia* and I, Omar, the Shariff-of-Sharon.

'Round and 'round I spun, Dervish to the dance. The dust funnel cloaked me, climbed my body, and leapt skyward.

Jody sprang from the porch, snatched up the garden hose, and soaked my high-blown fancies to mud.

"Why did you do that?" I sputtered, returning to earth with a thud.

"The music was shaking the glasses off the shelves."

Standing with the gushing hose in her hand, she asked, "What's today, odd or even?"

"I thought it was going pretty even until you turned the hose on me."

"No," she emphasized, shaking the hose as if she were choking a deadly snake and catching me in another splash of water and mud. "Is it an odd or even day?"

"Well, I'm okay but you're a little odd. Would you please stop soaking the grass. It's not our day. You're breaking the law."

"The grass is dying. My flowers are dying," Jody responded dryly. "If we can't water, we need rain." As if by command, low, black clouds raced to claim my sky.

Rain. My mind flooded with the horror. Not rain. Rain equals lawn mowing. The Lord taketh away, the Lord… I gawked at the newspaper she dropped on the porch. Jody couldn't be conjuring rain, could she? I counted myself lucky she didn't know the aboriginal rites of U-bach.

Travel the world from desert to rain forest. Make inquiries of medicine man or M.I.T. scientist. Few, save the rare anthropologist, witch, or former military school cadet will know the ceremony of U-bacci—the ceremony for making rain.

I was initiated into the rites in military school. The imperative—to drown out certain Sunday parades. The central icon of U-bach is the sacred U-bacci tree.

Perhaps you have seen a facsimile. They're more commonly known as newspaper trees by those ignorant of the dormant power unleashable through proper preparation and incantation.

When I first saw pictures of flooding in the Midwest, I suspected the worst. There are some forces of nature that must be handled with exactitude. Had someone deviated from the ritual of U-bacci?

The problem may have been the U-bacci tree itself. The ceremony requires a roll of local newspapers thicker than you'd use to hit a dog on the nose but smaller than a Sequoia. With razor blades—we used swords—slice down the length of the roll at half inch intervals, leaving four or five inches at the bottom to form the tree trunk. Tug at the center and extend the tree. Plant the base in the ground. The sliced strips hang like weeping willow branches. When surrounded by undulating, slam-dancing, painted bodies, the central spirit of the tree—its U-bach—takes pity on its supplicants and begins to weep torrents of tears that become rain.

It's all pretty simple, unless you don't know the proper body painting, or dances, or you use the wrong newspaper.

The newspaper must be precisely from the area to be rained on. If a Midwesterner had accidentally included regional papers...

Jody turned off the hose and went into the house. After a few minutes, she called out for me to check the recycle bin and gather up as many old editions of the *Advocate* as I could find.

I gulped.

"And bring me that box of razor blades from the garage."

Uh, oh. It's a hard rain's a gonna fall.

Small plane warnings
(1996)

Snow fell for the second day in a row and the third time in a week. News reports declared a new record for annual snow accumulation. I guided my trusty 1982 Ford Fairmont on a victory lap around town. She had carried me through the worst winter in recorded history. My confidence surged that together—man and machine—we would survive the approaching ice age.

When I returned home, the green light on my answering machine was blinking.

A message from Big Mama.

"A plane crashed. It was on the news. A small plane crashed and no one is answering the phone at you're brother David's house. Tell me the truth. I can take it."

David is my 42-year-old brother. Last year, he got a pilot's license and he bought a small plane. He and his wife, Nancy, are championship ballroom dancers. They use the plane to fly to competitions. There's one nearly every weekend.

I returned Big Mama's call but she was out, so I left a message on her machine. "Had to ditch over Sahara. Picked up by Bedouins. Will arrive U.S. by spring. Stop." Big Mama can't distinguish my voice from David's over the telephone. I thought the message would reassure her.

I was wrong.

I answered the phone on the second ring.

"Have you heard from your brother?" Big Mama wailed. "He just called. His plane crashed in the desert. When I heard it on the news, I knew it was him."

"That was me," I said.

"You don't have a pilot's license," she said.

"No, that was me on the telephone. I was only playing."

"Your brother crashes in the Sahara and you're playing?"

"The Sahara. That was me," I said.

"You don't have a plane and you don't have one of those walky-talky, cell-phone things. How could you call from the Sahara?"

"I didn't call you from the Sahara. David didn't call you. That was me on the telephone pretending to be him."

"You think I can't tell the difference between you and David, my own sons?"

"I know you can't."

"Have you talked to your brother?" she snapped. "I heard on the news. His plane crashed."

" 'A' plane crashed. Not 'his' plane crashed. Anyway," I reminded her, "David can't fly in bad weather."

"See, he's crazy with this pilot stuff. And now you tell me he can't fly in bad weather. So what was he doing flying?"

"He wasn't flying, " I said. "His license is restricted. He can't take off unless the weather is perfect."

"Since he got this plane, he flies here, he flies there. I'm worried all the time. Can you tell me honestly you know where your brother is?"

"Yes. He went to Cuba."

"Cuba?"

"Nothing dangerous. He was just going to drop leaflets over Havana. To advertise dance lessons."

"Son?"

"Yes, Mama."

"You were wrong when you said I can't tell the two of you apart."

"You can't."

"I certainly can. David's the one I like."

Fit as a fiddle
(1996)

Count down with me. Five. Four. Three. Two. One. And rest. Whew! Working my abdominals is tough. In fact, exercising all this old body's parts in the safety and privacy of my own home has proven to be a full-time occupation.

One night, as I was switching TV channels, I came across the AB-Roller infomercial. Like magic, two weeks later, the package appeared at my door. After what some have described as 'minimal assembly,' I was set to start my already-rolling abs t' rollin'. And roll 'em I did. Up, down. Up, down. Knees to the side and over and up. Strain and sweat. No pain, no gain. Up, down.

Before a week had passed, I'd ordered a heavy-duty stair-stepper to simulate heavy-duty stair climbing. And a small, plastic, single stair to simulate stepping from the street to the curb. A Nordic-style ski machine to simulate cross-country skiing through Norway. A stationary bicycle to simulate riding Uptown. And wrist weights to simulate picking up stuff.

As each apparatus arrived and was minimally assembled, I moved it into the guest room where I'd installed a TV and VCR so I could follow along with the professionals as they went through their exercise routines. I edited the videos together to create 'Ilan's Seamless Workout Session.' I covered the floor with color-coordinated exercise mats. Protection for my body. Pleasing to the eye.

Before I discovered ab-rolling, I pounded out three-miles-a-night running. Glendale to Summit, Billings, Cottage, Ames, Quincy, Pond, Beach, Gunhouse, Main, Oakland, Pleasant and School—three miles. I loved running. I loved the tidal wave of endorphins that broke over me and swamped my brain as I made the turn onto Cottage Street.

From there on, I felt like I was hoofing through heaven, feeling no pain, feeling no brain. The trouble is, people are supposed to feel pain.

A couple of years into runner's nirvana left me with a resting pulse of 50 bpm and the back of a 70-year-old. Even after the operation, the doctors said I'd never run again.

So, I tried cross-country skiing. Bought the skis, the poles, the shoes, and the lavender-on-black Spandex ensemble. With the first snowfall of the season, I blissfully embarked on a cross-country tour of my yard. An hour-and-a-half into swishing and sloshing and I'd negotiated the entire circumference of my acre-and-a-quarter holdings. I assessed my achievement, called my brother, David, and handed-me-down the entire outfit to him—skis, shoes, poles, Spandex ensemble.

The biking craze was made up of semi-cripples like me who had destroyed their bodies running and were now into low-impact exercise. But biking is more a mental exercise than a physical endeavor. Worrying about two tons of automobile slamming into 25 pounds of 10-speed bike is really a mind trip; and no matter how I envisioned the outcome of the collision, I couldn't describe any of them as low-impact.

Get out your pencils. Vehicle 'A,' weighing 2 tons and traveling north on South Main Street at a speed of 50-mph, slams into the back of vehicle 'B,' weighing 25 pounds, also traveling north but at only 20-mph. The driver of vehicle 'B,' weighing 160 pounds, is wearing a tear-shaped, plastic helmet. How many feet will rider 'B' fly through the air before he touches down, and how many minutes will elapse before he is officially pronounced dead?

In my house is a beautiful staircase made of Carolina Pine held together with pegs in a unique combination of wide and narrow treads. Some call it a work of art. Real stair-stepping means taking that staircase one-step-at-a-time, in socks. This is no exercise for the faint hearted. Climbing my stairs may be the most fearsome workout ever devised by man. One misstep, one slip on those beautifully crafted treads, can smash the coccyx of the unwary. Exercise on real stairs? Over my dead body.

So I roll my abs, twist my torso, and sweat like a monsoon downpour, all in the safety of my own padded room.

As I mindlessly pedal my stationary bike, worries of pitiless traffic bearing down on me don't slow me down. On my Nordic skier, nary a chance of launching into a fjord. I grunt and groan and strain my eyes to the mesmerizing blue light of the TV screen, secure in the knowledge that exercise, like great art, simulates life.

Man says 'no' to dog

(1994)

Each time the *Advocate* runs one of those 'adopt me' dog pictures, my wife, Jody, starts to bay at the moon.

Jody wants to adopt them all.

Not me. I recall the long canine line that has passed through our marriage. Dogs. Walk 'em in the rain dogs. Muddy paw prints on the floor dogs. Matted fur on the easy chair dogs. Drool on my suit dogs. Lawn unsafe for unshod walking dogs. And worse yet for ripple-soled running shoe dogs. Dogs and their endless variety of organically produced odors. The type of smells usually associated with year-old infants, hospital wards and, yes, dogs.

Read my lips. No more dogs.

But, there is only so much whining and scratching at the door of the heart a man can take. Especially if the whiner-scratcher is one's loving wife. So, on a sparkling Sunday afternoon, when the snow was melting and the streets were dry and all sensible people were drifting in napland, I borrowed friend Tom's four-legged beast for a test walk through the neighborhood.

Tom swears he got this dog from an animal shelter, but I think it must have been a fire chief's dog purloined in the night. I never realized how extensive a fire protection system the town has hooked-up.

With an ardor usually reserved for stage mothers dragging their children from audition to audition, Tom's dog dragged me from hydrant to hydrant, stopping at each as if to say, "Check this one out, Ilan. Looks like a little man with arms and a hat, doesn't it?" Then it was tug-tug-tug. "If you thought that one was great, wait until you see the one up the street." To me, they all looked the same. The dog must have thought so, too, because the snow around each plug received similar yellow stains of approval.

About fifteen hydrants into the tour de l'eau, the novelty was wearing a little thin. Tom's dog seemed to be slowing some himself. Suddenly he stopped and stood dead still in his tracks. His body stiffened. His legs stretched forward and back. His long floppy ears attempted to rise and twitch the way short-eared dogs' ears do. He pointed his shiny black nose toward the sky and sampled the passing scents in short whiffs. I saw his chest fill and heave a sigh as if he finally recalled the path to a well-loved plug around the bend.

The dog sprang into the air and shot forward to show me his prize. I was caught off guard and, before I could adjust to the force of his lunge, I was jerked off my feet, the dog dragging me down the street.

I flipped over onto my backside and caught enough ground to stop his forward motion. I was cut and bleeding. My best jeans had a hole torn out at the knee. It had taken three years to bring those jeans to the cusp of perfect comfort. I was dazed and angry. I'd had enough of dogs for a lifetime and I'd be dog-goned if I'd let him yank my chain one more step. I made it to my feet, steadied my balance, and defiantly stood my ground.

Tom's dog coughed, sputtered, and choked as he strained against the collar and leash. He dug his paws into the asphalt and pulled like Buck against the sledge, once again dragging me along the sanded road. So much for Nike running shoes. I made a mental note to call their office to ask if they make Determined Dog Opposition tread. But for now, it was wretched retching noises and off to see one more spigot.

Peter B. was power walking when we encountered him on Summit Ave. "Jody got her dog and you're on the leash." Peter laughed. (That's why nobody likes him.) "What make of mutt is that, anyway?"

I stopped and looked closely at Tom's dog for the first time.

Yech! He was a mess. Brown and white or white and brown, with sepia splotches where he was white and white reverses where he was brown. He had a wide, white circle around one droopy, bloodshot eye and brown around the other, with lots of dots and splots running down to his pink-ringed, gleaming, black nose.

He was more Picasso painting than dog. An amalgamation of spare parts and colors left over from the immortalized city bombed during the Spanish Civil War. "He's Guernican Dalmatian," I responded.

Peter B. nodded in recognition, as if that very breed had been on the tip of his tongue. "What's his name?" Peter B. asked, as he gingerly touched the dog's head.

I hadn't a clue. It had never occurred to me to ask Tom questions of pedigree and family who's-who. "Pablo," I answered. The designer of this piece-of-work dog must surely have been bombed out, one way or another.

Pablo and I finally arrived home to my yard where I thought I would introduce him to Jody and display my wounded body and jeans as anti-dog exhibits one through ten. No way, Jo-day!

Directly in front of our snowman, Pablo stopped to squat.

"Jody," I howled. "Jody! Come quick." Jody burst through the doorway. "Look," I sputtered. "D-D-Dog do." I pointed at the brown blemish on our white snow—"D-Dog did"—and its perpetrator, whose coat colors so perfectly matched the sepia tones newly painted at our snowman's feet.

It had never occurred to me that Pablo's color-scheme was, in fact, a billboard, a walking advertisement for his singular and perfect talent. Pablo was no mere Guernican Fire Hound. He was an accomplished impressionist in his own right. Still, I don't have to wait until the spring thaw to make up my mind about dogs. I turn up my nose at them.

You can't go home again

(1993)

Billy Peters dropped by the house a few days ago with his eight-year-old daughter, Beth, in tow. Beth stood at the living room piano and played a Mozart piano concerto. For a moment, I forgot that I was listening to a second grader play the familiar piece, then she hit a section she didn't know and began fingering trial-and-error notes, attempting to match the piano's sound to the tune in her head. After a while, she plopped herself next to Billy in the big easy chair and tucked herself up under his arm.

"Nice work, Beth," I said. "How long have you been working on that piece?"

"Hummphhhmm."

Billy gently slid her thumb from her mouth. "Come on, Beth," Billy urged quietly. "Ilan can't understand you if you're sucking your thumb."

"Mom showed it to me this morning," she replied, then slipped her thumb back in her mouth and snuggled in tighter against her dad.

"It's true," he said, as if in apology for the startling ability of his precocious offspring.

I watched Beth's forefinger curl over the bridge of her nose and wondered what music played in her head as her fingers stroked back and forth against her face.

Billy and Beth left. I started the Mozart piece on the CD player and settled myself into the oversized easy chair. My cat, Floyd, jumped up and nestled against me. Floyd purred in rhythm to the rise and fall of my chest. His soothing motor resonating near my heart, I closed my eyes, lost in the magic of the music.

From some long-tucked-away place in memory, I recalled having sucked my thumb as a kid. I rolled slightly in the chair and drew my knees up, reliving the sensation of absolute security, dreaming of my clown, Clarabelle, tucked under my arm while my fingers rubbed the cool, satin edge of my special blanket, remembering the hollow of my cheek that allowed my fingers to stroke around my nose and under my eye in time with the rhythms of sucking. And most of all, the memory of that perfectly shaped groove in the roof of my mouth, designer built by God for my thumb. After a rough day in the woods and swamps around Marie Avenue, a kid needed that security in his life.

Then came the day of reckoning, trauma day, the day my parents went for the South-of-the-Border solution—Jalapeño Day.

I remember it as if it were yesterday. Cold turkey! First my blanket was missing. Then Clarabelle, who hadn't been near clean water in the four years we'd been together, was presented to me fresh, clean, and fluffy from the washer-dryer. I put him up to my nose. Huh! Who was this impostor with the fresh scent? Where was the organic, loving, primeval-smelling, ecstasy-bearer of mold and grime whose aroma I needed to inhale to feel safe enough to sleep?

As I reached out my hands to the heavens in anger, anguish, and fear, two adults were on me in a surgically-accurate strike, attacking my thumbs—comforts of my life—with a liquid that made them tingle even as they were being swathed.

I stuffed the thumbs into my mouth—as much to protect them as to comfort me—but something was wrong. They'd turned against me. Instead of magical warmth, a different kind of heat was speeding from my mouth to my brain. Warmth turned to fire—fire to inferno. My brain sizzled in shock. Like Hamlet, betrayed, betrayed, betrayed. "O, I die, Horatio. The potent poison quite o'er-crows my spirit."

The Mozart finished. I startled awake in the silence. Winter night had overtaken the room. What had I been dreaming? Of a long-lost Clarabelle and a paradise lost?

My mind quickened. But why lost forever? No one was around. The house was still. Why not? I slipped my thumb into my mouth. Floyd rolled his head to watch me quizzically. Something was wrong. My teeth got in the way. They were too big. The last time I'd done this I'd been working off baby teeth. I'd gladly slip the Tooth Fairy a twenty if my teeth could be the way they were. The angle was wrong, the groove too wide. Why couldn't I have grown up with chubby fingers?

It was wrong—all wrong.

My left hand stroked Floyd's silky fur. He was purring near my heart.

I sat that way in the darkness for what seemed an hour, thumb in my mouth, index finger stroking between my nose and eye, all the while my left arm tightly hugging Floyd to my chest. I knew an important part of my life could never be retrieved. It was over. "Floyd," I said, "you can't go home again."

Perhaps sensing my loss, Floyd climbed to my shoulder and nestled against my face. I could smell the Friskies on his breath.

"Phew, Floyd, you smell like"—and then it struck me—"You smell like Clarabelle." And I gave him a big hug.

Maybe there is a way back.

Passing traffic
(1994)

I saw a man die at the airport once. I thought of him today. He wasn't the first person I'd seen die, nor was he the last, but I thought of him as I stood alone near the end of my driveway and watched the traffic passing on North Main Street.

On the day the man died, I'd gone to the airport to pick up my young niece and nephew who were to arrive on a flight from California. I was early and an airport security officer let me wait near the gate where the children would deplane. The area was empty and I chose a seat a few rows back from the concourse.

While I waited, another plane arrived at the gate. I watched the passengers hurry by. One of them, a man, broke pace with the crowd. I watched as he tripped and stumbled to the floor a few yards in front of me. Before I could react, he was surrounded by would-be helpers and curious onlookers. Someone began CPR. An ambulance crew arrived rolling a stretcher. The crowd parted to let them through. The paramedics placed the man on their stretcher and wheeled him away. I could see his shirt hanging open, the top of his pants undone. He was wearing red silk boxer shorts.

The crowd of passengers, the ambulance crew with the man, the would-be helpers and spectators, all departed. Once again, I was alone. The arrival door flew open and another stream of travelers rushed across the floor where, moments before, a man had died. I watched them as they hurried over the tiles. The airport resumed its normal business.

Last week, while I stood on the porch of my house, two cars collided on North Main Street. As I watched from the distance, the crash

played out as if it were a choreographed ballet. The sound of impact.
The awkward rotation of vehicles moving in a manner contrary to their
design. The delicate tinkling of glass shards landing on metal and
asphalt. Cars stopped and drivers ran to offer assistance.

One of the cars in the accident held four Sharon boys. I knew them
all. They were unhurt. The second car's single passenger, a man from
another town, was also unhurt. The police arrived. An ambulance and
EMTs appeared. Passing spectators slowed their vehicles to view the
scene. A tow truck was called in. The car containing the four boys was
badly damaged, the steel rear axle bent and mutilated by the impact.
The boys were nervous and shaken. The driver of the second car said
he was all right.

The father of the Sharon driver arrived. As he crossed the street to
his son, he visually assessed the violence of the impact, the damage
only inches behind the passenger compartment. He took his son by the
shoulders and held him at arm's length, looking into the boy's eyes.
Then he folded his son in his arms, rocking him from side to side. His
eyes were shut tight as he pressed his face to the boy's face and whispered in his ear.

Repairs were made at street-side and the out-of-town driver was
able to continue on his way. The ambulance left. The passengers left.
The spectators drifted away. The tow truck removed the boy's car and
the father walked his son back across the road, their arms still intertwined.

After directing traffic for a few minutes, the police officer returned
to his car and drove away. I stood alone at the end of my driveway and
watched as a new line of travelers passed along North Main Street.

A museum to live by

(1993)

I recall once asking my father's older brother, Jack, if he wouldn't like to visit the place where he spent the first ten years of his life. I remember his searing glare indicating the absurdity of my question. He had last seen that place, a village in Poland, in 1921. In the Holocaust, the Jewish village and most of its inhabitants were annihilated. It was on the same day I asked the question that I met one of my father's cousins for the first time.

We were both grown men. I already had a child. I knew that this cousin could tell me what others never had. He and I walked alone in my garden and I asked him how a survivor thinks about God. God, he said... his voice trailed off. Ilan, let me tell you about God. The Nazis came into the village and there was a big pit and they lined us up. I was nine years old, a few years older than your daughter. All the Jews were lined up and they were shooting us in the back of the head and we were falling into the pit. Then it was our family's turn. First, they shot my father in front of me and he dropped over the edge. My mother's arms were wrapped around me. They tried to pull me from her but she wouldn't let go. I heard the explosion behind me and I dropped into the pit with my mother on top of me and I could feel her blood and brains run into my mouth... I waited. I was in the pit covered over in bodies and I waited. When I thought it was safe, I dug my way up through the bodies and dirt. I don't know how I made it out but I got out and I had the taste of my mother's brains in my mouth. So when you ask me about God, I only know the taste of my mother's brains.

At the dedication of the U. S. Holocaust Memorial Museum, Elie Wiesel quietly and elegantly declared of the experiences of his youth, "It is not because I cannot explain that you won't understand. It is because you won't understand that I cannot explain."

I am forty-six years old and I tell you, understanding the Holocaust comes very slowly.

When I was a child, there was an adult secret being sorted out around me and what was known was not for the ears and minds of children. Who could tell children things too obscene and incomprehensible even for adults?

As a teenager with only mountains of raw statistical information, staggering numbers of bodies and eye glasses and fact-piled-upon-fact so that no human face could be put on them, I was consumed with anger and shame that European Jews, my people, could have behaved with such passivity and lack of fundamental survival instincts as to have allowed this slaughter to happen to them.

Allowed. I believed allowed. Like a rape victim allows. Six million allowed.

And in my sixteenth year, I went off to wander through Israel. I was with Israeli kids, eighteen-year-olds entering the army that year. Kids very much like me. And sometimes at night, we talked about Europe and the difference between them—The Victims, in some cases my friends' own parents—and us. We took it as an act of faith that such things could never have happened to us. And we didn't understand how 'It' had been possible.

Viewing our own youth and invulnerability, we assured each other that we didn't have tainted, cowardly genes. Those European Jews, with their centuries-old culture of practiced humility, must have rendered themselves complicitors to their own destruction.

Through detailed films like Shoah and the documentation of individual stories of survivors—like that of my friend Jack Pavony, liberated from Matthausen on May 6, 1945, a year and a half before my birth—we are able now to connect human faces with actual people. From the box cars filled with eyeglasses, shoes, and human hair, the masses dressed in striped jackets, we can now pick out individuals and distinguish their individual lives.

My friends and I have had to learn to stop blaming the victims for their failure to grasp the ungraspable, for not anticipating the incomprehensible, for being held hostages to love of children and devotion to parents and family. And the more I know of the victims' ordeals, the more I hear their individual stories, the more I'm able to tackle the staggering numbers one by one.

The Holocaust Museum permits us to look at the killers and the killed, to identify those countries and individuals who refused to go along and participate in separation and genocide, and who risked their lives to oppose it. The museum leads us to reflect on what is dark in the human experience as well as the inspiring hope and vitality of people who not only survived but lived, and dedicated themselves to pass on the story for themselves and for those unable to tell it.

The telling of their stories frees me and my children from thinking of them en masse as 'the Holocaust.' Even with respect to Germans and Poles, this museum of definition and experience tears down the barriers of 'we' and 'them.' That's an important breakthrough, for in the human experience, the verb 'to kill' is conjugated in reverse—it begins with 'them' and arrives home at 'me.'

As I think back to Israel thirty years ago, I wish that we could have understood that, exactly as those European Jews we rejected, we too could have been separated from our lives and loves by the nod of a head, the flicker of a flame; that some of us would have received or provided strength and hope to our fellows, and some of us would have done unspeakable things.

When people hear my cousin's story, often it makes them squirm. They want me to take it back, make it go away, say it's untrue. It makes me uncomfortable to tell it. But it is only one small piece in the jigsaw puzzle of millions of unspeakable stories that need to be spoken if we are to learn from them.

And will we ever learn?

Old friends and foggy nights
(1995)

There are nights when the fog rests thick on North Main Street and the sounds from passing cars are all but muffled to oblivion before they reach my door. On nights like those, when the hour is late and morning is closer than midnight, I slip into an old army jacket and sit out on my front steps to listen to the silence and feel the soft isolation in the fog. And sometimes I think about old friends.

Last night was like that.

Earlier in the evening, it had rained. I sat in my den by the yellow warmth of a desk lamp and rummaged through a carton of old photographs. Much of the history of my family is told in images found in that box. Some of the pictures were taken nearly a century ago. I worked to decipher faded inscriptions, some in Yiddish, some in Italian, written on the backs of photographs of relatives long dead.

I found pictures my father had mailed home during World War II, pictures of himself and his buddies in the landscapes of China and India. I could tell which pictures he sent home to his parents, and which were destined for my mother, by which language he chose to write his messages on the backs.

In the box were photographs taken at our house on Marie Avenue in the 1950s: a picture of a Fisher kid with a squirrel on his shoulder, my sister swinging a hula-hoop, and one of me and Blackie. I'm wearing a red cowboy shirt, Blackie has red-eye to match. The shot is out of focus. I brushed my fingers over the image of the dog in the photograph. "Hey, Blackie," I heard myself whisper in the empty den.

I rubbed my eyes. The rain had stopped. I put on my jacket and went outside to the porch. The amber lights of Main Street registered faintly through the fog and silhouetted the bare branches of the maples that form a barrier between my yard and the sparse traffic of civilization that passes by in the hours before dawn. Was it possible I'd not thought of Blackie for so many years?

Blackie had been part of me. He was born retriever, and I, human, but the difference was superficial. We were one breed, transcendent, a species apart. We shared a common language, ate the same food, slept in the same bed, and went everywhere together.

I got Blackie from Mr. Morse in 1952, the summer after our family came to Sharon. Blackie was a few months old, just weaned. I was five years. That's about the same age when you figure that we had to learn everything about each other and our new surroundings from scratch.

Those were the days before leash laws for dogs and fear of foul play for kids. Blackie and I were free, with freedoms no generation of kids and dogs that followed ours has ever known. We were free to go Uptown, down to the lake, free to follow the railroad tracks beyond the Heights in one direction and past the Box Company in the other. We were free to follow the brooks and explore the swamps. We roamed over Moose Hill as far as Route 1. On the way, we lay down on the moss and drank from tiny soaks of running water that came out of the ground. On the day the picture was taken, Blackie and I sat outside our house, alternating licks on a chocolate-covered ice cream, living the good life.

The 1950s brought a building boom to Sharon and Blackie and I made it our mission to inspect every construction site in town. Soon, we knew the carpenters by name and readily accepted snacks and lunch handouts as we made our treks. We spent afternoons jumping into newly dug cesspool holes, then fighting our way out against walls of crumbling earth. The sand pit on Farnham Road had giant, steep sides, perfect for jumping off, sliding down, or just sitting at the edge creating avalanches.

For the three years I attended the Pleasant Street School, Blackie walked me there in the morning, came back for recess, and was there again for the walk home at the end of the day. In the third grade, Blackie and I went to Hebrew School. I wanted him to join me in the classroom, but Mr. Shoham, the Temple Israel principal, refused to allow my friend to attend class. I argued that Blackie was Jewish, but the principal was from the old school. He refused dogs, even Jewish dogs, a proper Hebrew education. Mr. Shoham's edict became law when my father put his foot down. Blackie would either wait for me outside the school or be kept at home. So, three afternoons a week, and on Sunday mornings, Blackie lay outside my classroom window to keep an eye on me and pick up whatever education a dog could get from the outside looking in.

Blackie and I wrestled every day. Our bouts were a tangle of three pairs of legs and a set of arms. We rolled on the ground, jockeyed for position, growled, and bit each other. His favorite tactic was to slobber me into submission.

In our Superman period, we wore matching towel capes as we patrolled the neighborhood. I rode my bike and Blackie loped beside me.

Whenever he sensed trouble, Blackie pressed himself against my leg, ready to protect my flank and make the necessary stand in my defense.

In the summer of 1955, Blackie and I were separated for the first time. I went away to summer camp. Blackie couldn't come.

The long-ago images were clear in my mind as I sat on the stairs on North Main Street and looked out into the early morning fog. I remembered returning home, bursting through the door, calling Blackie's name. My mother put her arms around me and told me that Blackie had been attacked by an animal in the Marie Avenue swamp. She'd found him lying alone in the meadow across from our house and taken him to the vet. Nothing could be done to save him.

The street lights burned amber against the empty black limbs that border my yard. After forty years, I felt the press of Blackie's body against my leg, ready to protect my flank. I stared out at the fog and pulled my jacket tighter around myself.

"Hey, Blackie," I heard myself whisper into the empty night.

When you wish upon a star
(1993)

It was already 10 p.m. and a persistent overcast hovered above our house blotting out the sky and the promised meteor shower we'd hoped to see. Every few minutes since sunset, my son, Zev, stepped out onto the side porch to look skyward. Nothing. Not a single star, much less 'the greatest shower of shooting stars in a century,' was visible this night.

A moment later, Zev yelled into the house—a partial break in the cloud cover. I checked the sky. A few faint stars winked visible. With 'Let's go, Dad' burning in my son's eyes, we grabbed our cameras and headed for a dark, secluded spot behind the high school.

We'd prepared for this celestial event, calling a variety of camera stores for information on the best exposure times and settings to capture streaking extraterrestrials. The opinions we got were so astonishingly at odds with each other that we called the Kodak Company itself and spoke with a technician there. His recommendations seemed the most plausible.

We set our tripods in the field behind the school and checked our watches for timed exposures. Then we lay on the grass to scan the sky. Within a minute, a tiny North-South speck flittered through the night.

It may have been only a fraction as bright as a bottle rocket, but I can never feel blasé seeing a star streak across the sky. And in this case, it represented a small victory for science, good luck, and as the sky continued to clear, a hope of more to come. For Zev, this burning ember was the first shooting star of his life—a memory to last forever.

Watching the sky, I wondered how Zev would remember his star and this night. For me, the important images were being made lying on the grass, talking with my son.

A second star, brighter than the first, passed over us, East to West. With luck, we'd caught a souvenir photograph of a close encounter to mark its passing for, within an instant of entering our field of view, the celestial visitor burnt from existence, real now only in the luminescence of the images on our film and in our memories.

What is a comet's tail, after all, but specs of frozen dust that travel an orbit in space, spectacular only in their final moments as shooting stars, transitory and brilliant. So much like a photograph's sensitive particles transformed to image through the excitement of light. Or, the human mind's particles of chemistry that ignite our thoughts and emotions to memory—so much, in fact, like the human race itself, bits of dust on a spinning ball held in orbit around a star.

Zev's own passage is audible in the cracking of his voice as he discusses his next camera settings and the visions he's witnessed in the sky over our heads.

Traveling its 130-year rounds, the Swift-Tuttle Comet passed this spot in space and Earth's orbit only a few months ago. It is certain neither Zev nor I will encounter its return.

The shooting stars we see in the sky are the trailing hem of the comet's long tail. Earth will continue to pass through this bridal train annually as it has in years past. And my son, Zev, will continue to grow. His voice will become strong and steady. I hope he will always question his camera settings and all he encounters. But most of all, unlike the comet's train, I hope our relationship is not made of such transient material that, on its first contact with friction, it will burn and die. Instead, like the Swift-Tuttle itself, each pass will bring us closer together.

We saw thirty shooting stars this night, Mr. Cricket—that's thirty wishes, please.

One more wish, please, Mr. Cricket

Pa, Paa!

*Even the effects of grime and neglect
could not diminish its
architectural beauty*

One man – One vote

Fisher & Dylan, no spring chicken

This winter is Jolson

(1994)

'If you don't like New England weather, wait a minute.'

I don't know who said that first but it may well have been Dylan the Rooster, the copper weathervane who sits up on my roof.

It's Dylan's job to point out which way the wind blows. I think of him as the Bruce Schwoegler of North Main Street. But even the usually reliable Dylan is crooning a different tune this weird winter.

The other morning, as I walked out onto the front porch, I heard singing drifting down from Dylan's cupola. I decided it was time to pay him a visit and get to the bottom of our weather problems. I placed a ladder against the side of the house and climbed to the rooftop for a heart-to-heart with the fickle fryer.

When my head cleared the fascia board, Dylan was nowhere in sight but the sound of singing came from his room. "I'm sittin' on top-top of the world, just rollin' a-long, rolling a-long...."

"Dylan," I demanded as I pounded on his louvered roost. "I can't believe you're still in bed. You can bet Dick Albert isn't sacking out when there's weather happening. Do you realize what's been going on out here? This is the worst New England weather since... since...," I had to think for a moment, "...since the last worst New England weather."

I recapped. "One morning, the temperature was below freezing, by noon it was over fifty degrees, then it rained cats-and-dogs. What's happening here?"

Dylan poked his head out of his cupola, flipped on his Victrola, and started to sing along with the scratchy voice on an old 78 record.

"Though April showers may come your way, they bring the flowers that bloom in May...."

He cocked his head the way roosters do and winked at me.

"Don't get brassy with me, Dylan. Remember, I'm the one who provides you with this room with a view. Are flowers in May your answer to New England's weather woes? Well, for your information, it's now February and last night it snowed tiny ice crystals the texture of Domino's sugar."

Dylan dropped to one knee, spread his wings in a gesture of supplication, and gave forth, "The sun shines east the sun shines west...."

"That's right, Dylan," I interrupted. "But, while the sun was shifting east to west, the temperature was jumping up and down like the balance in my checkbook."

"There's a rainbow 'round my shoulder, and a sky o' blue above...."

"That was two days ago. Then we got eight more inches of snow and no school again."

"Let it blow and storm. I'll be warm, 'cause I'm in love...."

"Well, I'm happy you're warm and lovey. But those sudden melt-offs are causing ice dams. Water is leaking into people's houses."

"Go down to the levee, I said to the levee...."

"Dylan, I don't understand you. Since when are you an Al Jolson fan? I thought you were into folk-rock. You used to be a rooster with a social conscience." I looked skyward and felt a shiver pass through my body. "Dylan, is that a nor'easter moving in?"

"When there are gray skies, I don't mind the gray skies. You make them blue, Sonny Boy...."

"Don't Sonny Boy me, you fair-weather fowl. I want to know when this crazy winter will end."

"When the red-red-robin comes bob-bob-bobbin' along, along. There'll be no more sobbin' when he starts singing his own sweet song...."

"Wake up! Wake up, Dylan!" I shouted

"All right! Take it, Ilan! Wake up, wake up, you sleepy head. Get up, get up, get out of bed...."

"Dylan, I don't want to sing Jolson. I want a good weather forecast for the people of New England. Or at least some advice on what to do."

"When the wintry winds start blowing, and the snow begins to fall... da, da, da, da, da, da... California, here I come...."

"California?" I gulped. "California! Dylan, don't you know what happens in California? They don't just have bad weather, they have earthquakes."

Obviously Dylan hadn't heard about The Big One. He'd been too busy packing preening oil and Coppertone for his winter vacation at Universal Studios.

"Right back where I started from...."

I felt hurt, abandoned by my too vain vane.

"See you around, Dylan," I snapped, "I'll take New England weather over earthquakes in California anytime."

Dylan whirled on his arrow.

"Ilan, is that all you have to say to a pal who's off for a well deserved winter escape to sunny Southern Cal?"

"If you're intent on flying the cupola when I need you here with me, then you deserve California, and it's Toot-Toot-Tootsie good-bye."

Home on the firing range
(1993)

Billy Peters decided he wanted to join me at the Sunday morning tin-can plink down at the gun club firing range. He went to get the necessary gun permit and this is what he told me when he returned:

That's a rough test. I told the Sergeant at the desk I wanted a permit to buy a gun. He reached under the counter, handed me a permit application form on a clipboard and told me to have a seat and fill it out.

I looked at the form. There was only one question. I didn't expect a lot of questions. Americans have the right to own guns and all, except maybe convicted felons or something. But the question they asked was, 'Do you believe in God?'

Well, I didn't think they could ask for that type of personal information. When I read it, I thought it was one of those trick questions. And, judging by the way the Desk Sergeant stared at me, I said to myself, 'Billy, you're in trouble now.'

I mustered my courage, walked up to the desk and told the Sergeant, "This is America, I don't have to answer this."

"Okay," he said and took the clipboard away. He sat down at his desk. I stood waiting for about five minutes. He was reading the newspaper.

"Excuse me," I interrupted. "Can I get my permit now?"

He looked up. "What kind of permit?"

"The gun permit."

The Sergeant reached under the counter, pulled out the clipboard and told me to have a seat and fill out the form. I looked at the Sergeant and the form and quickly circled 'YES' and handed it back to him.

The Sergeant stared at the form for a long time and gave me a rough looking over, too; then he asked if I was sure that was how I

wanted to answer the question. I nodded. He told me to sign and date
the form. I did that and handed it back to him. Again, he studied it for
a long time. Then he reached under the counter and—Thwack!— he
stamped it 'REJECTED' in big red letters.

"Hey wait a minute," I protested. "You can't do that."

"Move away from the counter and keep your hands in the clear
where I can see them," the Sergeant ordered. His right hand slowly
unsnapped the safety strap on his holster.

"I don't understand," I protested, backing away. "I wrote I DO
believe in God."

"That right, sir—Rejected."

I started back toward the counter.

"Easy there, son," The Sergeant said, his hand resting on the handle
of his gun. "Please move back away from the counter and don't make
any sudden moves. You one of those Waco-Whackos?"

I shook my head, no.

"Islamic Mental-List?"

"No... I'm..."

"Ulster Catholic IRA?"

"Sir." I was shaking my head.

"Protestant Agent Orange Squad?... Jewish Offense League?...
Serbian Orthodox Ethnic Cleansers?... Militant Unitarian?"

"No, sir, I don't believe in killing."

His gun was halfway out of its holster. "I knew it. You're a
Womber-tomb-er?"

"What's that?" I asked.

"You know, a doctor-killing pro-lifer?"

"Sir...?"

"Christian Scientific American Bomber?... American Friends
Society Plastique League?... Hindu Hitmen?... Armed Amish Army?...
Guns and Rosaries?"

"Sergeant, I'm not any of those things!"

"Son, you DO believe in a supreme being, don't you? You wrote it
right here." He pointed at the form with the muzzle of his gun. "Well,
who do you want to kill?"

I swallowed hard. "Sergeant, I lied on that form. There is no God."

The Sergeant pointed his pistol directly at my forehead. "Are you
sure, son? Think carefully now."

"Sure as shootin'," I stammered.

The Sergeant waved his gun for me to approach the counter. "Fix the form and sign it." Sweat was running down my face as I wrote on the paper. I closed my eyes and slid the clipboard back across the desk. I felt a cold, hard touch on my forehead. Smack! The Sergeant kissed me right between the eyes.

His lips were still touching my forehead as he spoke. "Thank God for a non-believer." Tears were running down his cheeks as he handed me the gun permit.

"Son, one word of advice. It's praise the Lord and pass the ammunition out there. But there's one thing you can be sure of."

"Sir?"

"There are no atheists in foxholes, son, and that makes my job a whole lot safer. Bless you, boy."

Family in high places
(1995)

The winter thermometer plunged to sixty-five degrees. I built a small bonfire out in the yard to burn off the year's accumulation of brush and tree limbs. I threw a branch on the fire and watched as the flames worked their way into the wood. Actually, the true purpose of my annual brush burn is to look like I'm doing something productive while I toast marshmallows on a stick.

The composition of the standard marshmallow ball has undergone significant change over the years. I'm forced to spend an inordinate amount of quality fire time perplexed as to what adjustments I should make in the distance between marshmallow and flame, and the precise angle of stick to fire, to achieve a perfect, brown hue on my marshmallows and then pull them from the fire before they prematurely flame-out into carbon goodies.

The marshmallow bag was definitely half empty when Dylan, the copper rooster weathervane who lives in the cupola on the roof of my house, let out a spine-chilling yowl. I dropped my stick and ran for the house.

Dylan strained on tip toes, his arrow pointing East. Frantically he flipped his head from side to side so his off-set eyes could catch a movement in the distant sky that had caused his alarm.

The sky darkened. The ground trembled. And like a screeching tornado, a wing-to-wing formation of six fighter planes dove toward my house. They blackened the sky over Dylan's perch. The wake of after-burners flipped Dylan around on his arrow so fast that the sound of his squawk was lost in the whoosh of rushing air.

"There, Ilan! There!" Dylan gasped when he finally stopped spinning. "Did you see them? Metal birds! Metal birds like me. Help me get out my genealogy chart. I think they're from my mother's side of the family." Dylan ducked into the cupola and scrambled through his library.

"Those were fighter planes, Dylan. Not weathervanes."

"What's the difference? They're metal. They fly!"

"They're not like you. They're made of lightweight alloy, not copper."

"I thought they looked a little pale. I'll bet they don't get enough sun. I'll call and invite them over for lunch. They're awfully big. Do you think your roof can hold them?"

"Dylan, they were fighter planes. Air Force F-15s. I don't know why they were flying so low over Sharon."

"Low! They must have been a thousand feet up. I didn't know anyone from my mother's side could fly that high."

"Dylan, they're not related to you. Men get inside and fly those planes. They wear special gravity suits. When they push the pedal to the metal, they can fly more than two thousand miles an hour. Planes like those flew in Desert Storm."

"I was in the nor'easter of '94. I spun so fast I pulled three G's without a suit. How's that for combat flying?" Dylan ducked into his cupola and didn't show comb or feather for fifteen minutes. When he finally hopped back on his arrow, he looked a bit down in the beak.

"Everything okay?" I asked.

"I was on the horn with the head of Ops down at Otis."

"Did you ask why those planes buzzed the treetops over Sharon?"

"The 'Eagles' were practicing a bombing run."

"Over Sharon? Over my house?"

"Oh, forget that, Ilan. That's not the important stuff. He said the Air Force won't let me enlist."

"I'm not surprised. You're a weathervane."

"Damn right, I'm a weathervane! I told him I logged four years air time over the last four years, half of it night duty, and I come from a long line of flyers. I had relatives in the air long before Amelia or

Lindbergh. Heck, my cousin gave Herman Wouk the title *The Winds of War*. But when I told him I was a rooster, he said, 'You mean I'm talking to a chicken?'

"A chicken, Ilan. Imagine. I've been doing weather recon my whole life. And, except for scarfing down the odd pizza, I'm more fuel-efficient than any bird in the air. I give a hoot and don't pollute. Nobody who sits up on a roof year 'round in New England is a chicken."

"Listen, Dylan, now that the cold war is over, lots of good aircraft are grounded. It's no reflection on you. Modern fighting equipment requires speed and stealth."

"Speed and stealth? Watch this."

I watched for more than a minute but Dylan didn't move a feather. "What am I supposed to see?"

"I can make your bag of marshmallows disappear."

I looked back toward the fire. The marshmallows were right where I left them.

"Gotcha!" Dylan said, and hopped off his perch. We sat by the fire together and roasted marshmallows on sticks.

"You know, Ilan, I told that officer that roosters have been going to war for thousands of years. It doesn't seem fair to keep me out of the service."

"Dylan, better watch what you say. They may enlist you as chicken salad."

Dylan's comb began to twitch. Suddenly the sky thundered again with the roar of F-15s. A voice filled the air around us. Dylan's copper body was acting as a radio receiver. "This is Eagle Team Leader calling Dylan. Do you read me, Dylan?"

"Eagle Leader, this is Dylan. I read you five-by-five."

"Dylan, when we flew over earlier, I saw you doing weather recon on the roof. Are you my second cousin Tillie's boy?"

"Tillie is my mom. That's an affirmative."

"I thought I saw the family resemblance. Just to let you know, when our weather satellites pass over Sharon, they take wind readings from your arrow. You've got a whole lot of family up here depending on you and we appreciate the job you do for us."

"Just my duty, Eagle Leader."

"Hold on, Dylan. I've got something coming in over my computer. Langley analysis says you're holding your marshmallow too high over the flame. Correct with a fifteen degree drop in attitude. That's it for now, Cuz. See you the next time we're over Sharon."

Dylan signed off and adjusted the angle of his marshmallow to the flame. Sure enough, it toasted up brown as copper. Even in the world of weathervanes, it's good to have family in high places.

Cry for me Argentina
(1997)

I'm sick.

I'm so sick. I moved into the guest room. I closed the door to family and friends. I set up the humidifier by my bedside and arranged tinted, brown bottles containing elixirs that have to be measured out by the teaspoon or capfull. I set out ranks of safety-topped, amber vials filled with decongestant capsules and horse-sized scientific-breakthrough antibiotics of various-milligram potency, to be swallowed with food or milk, the latter of which I'm intolerant of, and which require flushing with such-and-such number of glasses of liquid, which number, when taken cumulatively over a ten-day period, would fill a child's plastic-frog swimming pool.

I'm sick.

Chicken soup in massive quantities sick. Chicken soup made with entire chickens, shopping baskets full of chickens, a gaggle of Frank Perdue's finest, boiled one after another in giant pots, with onions and carrots, and thickened with delicate, baby pastina, and served in green-and-white striped French breakfast bowls laid out on pale-green serving trays with hospital-white cloth napkins and silverware placed just so, and all prepared, arranged, and delivered to the sickbed by my loving nurse, Jody, who fluffs the pillows behind me and stands ready to feed me, spoonful by spoonful, should my strength falter, and all performed with the proper look of grave concern displayed on her brow.

I'm sick.

And I'm in pain. My aching digits barely able to negotiate the child-proof containers that encase the healing potions. So wracked with pain that a bottle of some-tussin-or-other slips from my fingers and bounces from knee to shin to foot, setting off competing points of agony that send my cerebral cortex into sensory overload, flipped-out like a shorted breaker that shoots off white-hot sparks that my jaw interprets as a mouth-full of cavities in need of emergency services, causing a sneeze that folds me in half then shoots me back upright again.

I'm sick.

Sick in the way that only men can be sick. Sick past the experience of women. Warrior sick. Prop me up against a tree with the last grenade sick. Shoot me sick. Eschew the blindfold. Tempted to take the offered last butt, but will settle for a thermometer, if you can shake it down for me, please, Dear.

I'm sick.

Shallow watery breaths sick. Slow beats through the carotid. Lost count at twenty. Decaffeinated tea with honey? Yes, Honey. Close the door, but don't wander far. I need rest, rest, sleep.

Oh, I'm sick.

Physical training at the peak
(1997)

I sat on my front steps, a morning cup of coffee in hand. Over the past few days, the growth of spring leaves had all but erased Main Street from view. Azalea and dogwood blooms accented the scene in splashes of red, pink, and white against the tender, green leaves of the maples. The smell of lilac sweetened the air.

I closed my eyes and tried to recall the bleak, bare views of a few weeks ago but the scent of lilac held those winter scenes at bay and I was returned, helpless captive to the beauty of spring.

My rapture was broken by the putt-putting sound of a Volkswagen bus as it circled the drive and pulled to a stop in front of me. The driver popped out of the van and grabbed for my hands.

"Must be Ilan," he said, clutching my hands in his bony fingers. "I'm Herbie. Here for Dylan."

I slipped one hand free and pointed toward the roof.

"In the cupola, is he?"

I nodded.

Herbie dashed behind the garage and returned seconds later with an extension ladder. He threw it against the house and scampered to the rooftop.

I looked at the rusty Volkswagen and tried to visualize the spring scene beyond but it was gone. Even the scent of lilac was masked by gas and oil fumes. Beauty is so transient, I thought. Change the only absolute in the universe.

I sighed, gathered up my cup and went into the house for my morning shower.

When I completed my regime de toilet, I looked out the window. The bus and its wiry driver were gone. I stepped out onto the porch. The ladder was still against the house.

I climbed up to speak with Dylan.

"Ilan, that you?" North Main Street's most affable weathervane called as I cleared the peak of the roof. "I'll be with you in a jiffy."

Dylan hopped out of his cupola, running a towel over his handsome rooster body. "I was in the shower," he said. "I'm just drying off."

"Who was that guy?"

"Herbie? He's my personal trainer." Dylan leapt onto his perch and rotated with the wind until he was facing North. "How's my profile?"

"Personal trainer? Personal trainer? Who ever heard of a weathervane with a personal trainer?"

"No pain, no gain," he said. "Can't pinch an inch on this bird. Frank Perdue, eat your heart out. And Ilan, speaking of eating your heart out, what are you growing there, the soft underbelly of Europe?" He did a quick North-South flip, then flipped back facing North again. "Nice patina, huh?"

"What's it cost you to have that guy come to the house?"

"I'm his first rooster. Heck, I'm his first copper. I told him I could get him in with the big whale weathervanes. Lots of whales on the rooftops of Sharon. Lots of blubber. So, I'm like a special deal. I'm supposed to tell my friends."

"Dylan, how do you come to have a personal trainer?"

"Where have you been, boy? 'Everyone' who's 'anyone' has a personal trainer. How do you work out?"

"I don't."

"My point, exactly." Dylan smiled and did a pair of 360-degree flips. "Weather-vaning is a high-stress occupation. I'm on this arrow rain-or-shine, morning, noon, and night. How about that lighting storm the other day? I had to hang on for dear life."

"Wait a minute. As I recall, you were in your cupola listening to Windham Hill environment CDs."

"The unkindest cut of all. You said I could have the night off. You said you were going to bed. Besides, who in their right mind would go out in a storm just to see which way the wind is blowing? And, as I recall, before I went on that vacation to the Catskills last year, I gave you Dick Albert's private beeper number in case you needed an emergency weather update?"

Dylan was right.

"A well-toned chicken never fowls up." He cocked his head right and left to get a good look at me. "Work the pecks," he said and bobbed his neck up and down while he did push-ups on his perch. "Those are chicken work-out jokes. For my video."

"Video?"

"Which came first, the chicken or the sheet metal?"

I laughed.

"Ilan, you love me."

"Sure, I love you."

Dylan hopped into my arms, squeezed me in his wings, threw his head back and let out a double cock-a-doodle-doo. As his call echoed back from Moose Hill, he whispered in my ear, "You're no spring chicken. I can get you a good deal from Herbie. What do you say?"

"Dylan, did I ever tell you that when I work up a sweat, I get an overwhelming craving for duck sauce?"

Grass clipping: a growth industry
(1993)

Alison, a high school junior, knows a good business opportunity when she sees one.

Her mother was nearly struck dumb when Ali offered to take over the lawn-care responsibilities this summer. The startled mom agreed to pay her teen-age daughter the same $25 rate she'd paid a lawn service last year.

With the $25 firmly committed, Alison phoned Michael, college wrestler, martial-arts student, and body builder. She put her proposal to him and he agreed to perform the summer lawn duties for $35 per mowing. They arranged a time on Saturday for the first clipping.

Alison's next calls were to her junior-class girlfriends inviting them for Saturday brunch.

When Saturday rolled around, the lawn and porch were crowded with luncheon invitees. Alison was serving the microwave hors d'oeuvres when Michael made his first pass across the lawn. Halfway through the second swath, Michael stopped and stripped off his shirt. Ali nudged a few of her friends to check out the wrestler's bod.

Boom! A junior-class-nuclear-blast chain reaction passed through the lunchers faster than neutrons at critical mass.

Like stranded sailors sighting distant sails, young ladies hung from the railings, whistling and waving as Michael's body glistened in the sun. He smiled and waved back, strategically turning the mower on the next tack to afford his fans the best view of his wrestler's pects.

When Michael finished mowing, he stood near the porch and slowly wiped the sweat off his body with his shirt. The only sound on the summer air was the clinking of ice cubes against orthodonture. Michael put the lawn mower in the garage and drove away. The force of the collective exhale from the porch was so palpable on the air that leaves stirred three streets away.

Alison offered a suggestion: Why not keep the class together over the summer with a luncheon every other week. Alison would schedule them for the times when Michael or one of his friends was mowing the lawn. The girls were all for it.

After all, one girl chimed in, what a great way to keep up school spirit over the summer. Ali suggested everyone tell a friend.

They all nodded in agreement. Then Alison broached the subject of expenses. How about if everyone chipped in $5, half the price of a movie when you figured in both the food and entertainment. Someone giggled and asked if five would be enough. Alison said she thought it would. Soon she was holding a fistfull of five-dollar bills.

Alison's forty-something mom and her best friend Ellie had been watching the lawn-mowing activities from an upstairs window. After the girls left, Alison told her mom that she would be hosting class luncheons on a regular Saturday schedule throughout the summer— good for school spirit and all. The two baby-boomer women look at each other, and Alison, catching a peculiar glint in their eyes, asked if they and some of the other mothers would help out by preparing the menu. The women smiled and patted Alison's hand, promising any assistance necessary for a wholesome, school-related activity.

That night Alison sat at her desk and deducted her expenses from her take. She found that she'd cleared twenty dollars for herself. She'd plow that money back into the business and easily parlay her profit as long as nature continued to cooperate—and she had a gambler's feeling it would.

As for her mother's eagerness to help, that hadn't been lost on Alison at all. The young entrepreneur's head hit the pillow already planning her expansion into the promising and lucrative 'Mom's Friends' market. In the morning, she'd call her partner Michael and see if he could arrange for a crew of wrestlers to wash windows for the growing list of mothers she envisioned queuing-up to scribble their names across her balance sheet.

On loan

(1993)

The wide-eyed full moon sank in the western sky over Pleasant Street. From the east, the dawn spread gray across North Main, pushing hard against the past. The taxi had come in moonlight and gone with the dawn, carrying my precious cargo away from home, away from me, back to her life in the nation's capital.

Her bags, overloaded with winter clothes and favorite books chosen from the shelves and closets of her past, were far too heavy for her tiny frame to manage. The taxi man grunted as he placed them in the trunk.

Jody and I closed the cab door and pressed our fingers against the window glass. Our daughter touched back and the taxi pulled away. She'd only been on loan for the long holiday weekend.

A trash truck clanked curbside as the taxi disappeared from view. The sound of scrunching Hefty bags with their contents of turkey carcass and fixin's punctuated the end of Thanksgiving and the return to anyday.

The town felt empty, her tiny presence departed. Once, it seemed she'd be ours forever. Now she was grown and gone.

I'd been her father at her age, born wiser in a simpler time. I didn't feel so wise now as I wrapped my arm around Jody and returned to the house.

The sprawling, thirteen-year-old Zev moved quietly through the upstairs hallway casting a wistful look inside his sister's room. Only a residual pile of clothes and a hollow feeling marked her coming and going.

The trash truck, with its crunch-and-whine, worked its way toward the square, busily compacting the debris of holiday times: of Thanksgiving dinner, a houseful of family and friends, and the return of our daughter's high school class of 1988, all compressed into memory.

Zev went off to school. I went back to bed. By the time I awoke for the second time, the sun was high in the sky. My red-headed woman-child would be back at her desk on Pennsylvania Avenue, only a block from the most powerful space on the planet.

Our Thanksgiving roller-coaster ride began on Wednesday morning when an 8:30 arrival at Logan delivered first-born Fisher-kid, Tamara, home from her fast-track, inside-the-beltway life, to the nurturing serenity of home and hearth, fully prepared to consume the six basic food groups of America's homecoming holiday—turkey, stuffing, mashed potatoes, cranberry sauce, pie, and seconds.

This was also reunion weekend for Tamara's high school class of 1988. Five years out of town, most friends who dropped by the house seemed eager to mingle, dredge, crow, and cry. The town's lovely children returned to old friends, strangers in a familiar mold. Some brought significant others. Others brought others less significant. Laughing, giddy and giggling, they touched the safety and innocence of childhood once more for a few short hours before leaving, returning to their other lives. The next morning wore a tinge of sadness at the realization of return and returning and the inevitable emptiness we feel.

The once-babies of the town had migrated home with the season. They'd eaten, loved, laughed, and departed. All that remains are the usual scattered papers the trash men have missed and the idea scrunching in my chest that every new season is bitter-sweet at best.

We'll always have Paris
(1995)

Hollywood lifted the lid on its King Oscar nominees last week and, judging from the look of these brislings, the waters have been over-fished. All they've produced is Pulp, Gump, and-a-Funeral.

Every year, with the predictability of Thanksgiving and the yahoo of Super Sunday, Hollywood announces its Oscar nominees. But, where a football team needs to survive obstacles, injuries, and a schedule of killer opponents, all the competitors for this year's Oscar-quest were belly-up long before the season started.

When the pilgrims declared Thanksgiving in 1621, the holiday was the Irving R. Thalberg Lifetime Achievement Award of its day. "In thanks for our survival, good hunting, and a sustaining harvest—may I have the envelope please? And the winner is...God. Accepting on behalf of God is Charlton Heston."

While the film industry rewards some of the same qualities as the NFL and the Pilgrims, those early Massachusetts folk didn't declare another Thanksgiving until 1630, nine years after the first.

Hollywood could take a lesson from the Pilgrims' play book and present awards only when it accumulates a sufficient supply of outstanding pictures, or produces at least one picture significant enough to warrant celebration.

This year's odds-on favorite to take the Oscar for best picture is *Forrest Gump*. I don't think the movie deserves an Oscar, but I thought it was a cute film that should be nominated for a Betty Booper Award.

The Oscars should be run like Hall of Fame inductions.

Five or more years should pass between a film's release to theaters and its eligibility for an award. All eligible films would be thrown into competition together and, like baseball players, some will win Oscars in their first outing. Others will never win.

In 1962, *Lawrence of Arabia*, *The Miracle Worker*, *To Kill a Mockingbird*, *The Longest Day*, *Divorce Italian Style*, and *David and Lisa* all hit the big screen. Lawrence won best picture. But, how would Gump fare against the losers? Tough fight right down the line. In '83, *Terms of Endearment*, *Tender Mercies*, *The Year of Living Dangerously*; '82, *Ghandi*, *On Golden Pond*, and *Reds*. To match this year's crop against the pix of the past, I need to paraphrase the great philosopher, Seuss—thump, thump, thump, Gump goes bump.

After reviewing the list of this year's nominees, Jody, Zev, and I went to see a real movie.

At the Orpheum Theater in Foxboro, we stopped at the candy counter for drinks and popcorn, then found seats at a corner table at Rick's Cafe Americain in *Casablanca*.

On the big screen, in living black and white, Sam played a little something on his piano as Ingrid Bergman and Paul Henreid walked by. Wow! Of all the gin joints in all the towns in all the world, they walked right into the Orpheum. On the other side of the cafe, I heard Claude Rains admonish Bogey, "How extravagant of you, throwing away women like that. Someday they may be scarce." Tell 'im, Claude.

I didn't need more brains than a hill of beans to know trouble had come to Casablanca when the patrons at Rick's rose in song, under the musical direction of Victor Laszlo, with a wink and a nod from Rick, and sang *La Marseillaise* with enough volume, verve, and joie de vivre to drown out Major Strasser and his all-Nazis chorale. Round up the usual suspects. I've seen *Casablanca* fifty times and have still never found a dry eye in the house during that scene. Here's lookin' at you, kid.

In real life, the colorized version of real life, Franklin Roosevelt ordered the 1943 Academy Award winning *Casablanca* played for his guests at the White House a week before he went to meet Churchill in—where else—Casablanca. The Nazis intercepted a cable prior to the conference, but failed to understand that the meeting place was Casablanca, North Africa, and not The Casa Blanca, Washington, D.C. Major Strasser had blown it again.

In the black and white version, Strasser got a bullet in the belly. Ilsa Lund and Victor Laszlo caught the plane to Lisbon. Sam played it for her, then played it again for him. Louie dumped the Vichy water in the trash and, arm-in-arm with Ricky, left to join the Free French at Brazzaville.

Heck, this year they served us up Pulp and Gump, but we'll always have Paris.

Gonzo with the wind
1994

The other day, on the steps of the public library, I met a woman whose name chivalry forbids me to reveal. She was reading a book written completely in dialog. Not one descriptive paragraph intruded between mouth, ear, and eye. In this book, all the female characters spoke in coy, southern inflection; the men were virile, strong, and sensitive. It was a paperback, one of a series by this author, and it appeared the cover illustrator left art school sometime before learning to draw men's shirts.

My friend, the reader, sat on the library steps because she could read one of these page-turners in two-hours-and thirty-five minutes, give or take five minutes, and, being close by the library door, she could finish a book, close the cover, get up, go inside, return the empty, and be back on the steps with a refill before you could say "scan my card" six times in rapid succession.

The series, she explained, was set in the time of The War Between the States, a war we here call The Civil War. But, she assured me, those Yankee blue coats were not at all civil in their manners and were sorely lacking in propriety and proper education in how to treat ladies of refinement, and so, for the heroines to refer to the war as The War Between the States was understandable even to her, born and bred as she was, in the North, on Pleasant Street—South Pleasant Street, she reminded.

A war between states is a much more civilized affair than a war between people, didn't I think? And speaking of affairs, well, you have your affairs of state, which is what the war was about, and affairs of the heart, which is the true underlying theme of these heart thumpers that create civil war between inhaling and exhaling and bring a flush to your cheeks, a trace of moisture to your lip, and a tug deep down in the pit of your stomach, she explained, her gaze drifting off into the distance toward the belfry of the old town meeting house.

The reader, a holder of a fistful of advanced degrees from some of Boston's most prestigious institutions of higher learning, said the only diploma she regretted not taking was for the Evelyn Wood speed-reading course, because the writer of her series, a certain Pierre de la Fonte, of the New Orleans de la Fontes, could turn out a new book every hour and twelve minutes, around the clock, which meant try as she might—and she was trying mightily—she would never catch up on the up-to-the-minute comings and goings of Ashley.

I didn't know if Ashley was hero, heroine, or horseflesh but I assumed, by the way she caught little gasps of breath after she spoke the name, that he was the former.

Of course, she said, he's the former, a farmer, former owner of a small plantation, dispossessed because he opposed slavery, ostracized by his fellow planters, forced, as punishment, into the fields to do manual labor, bull labor. But, even under the lash, his proud back never stooped, his tired, aching muscles never sagged, and every night after dark, the sister of the evil plantation owner who enslaved him came in the darkness, to his tar shack, and massaged chaste hope into his all but unconscious body. And before morning light, she slipped away, having never allowed him to see her face or hear the sound of her tender voice.

The reader turned her burning gaze on me. I thought she would sweep me into her arms right there beside the statue of Deborah Sampson. But I had misjudged.

So, Blue Belly, what do you say to that kind of love?

There I was, caught between two women—one bronze, the other a would-be Georgia peach.

Well, frankly, my dear, I don't give a damn.

Twenty-five years, but who's counting
(1994)

Jody and I have been married for twenty-five years. That's a quarter of a century. That's more than half the years we've been alive. Looking forward from our wedding day, twenty-five years was forever. Looking back, it was no time at all.

Maybe we really did marry for forever. We said so at the time. Well, kind of, in a fingers-crossed sort of way. I mean, it was forever, unless things didn't work out. Forever, unless we learned we weren't right for each other, rattled each other's nerves, drove each other crazy, argued, didn't have fun. It was forever, except for the million or so hedges that gave us the right to part as friends and go our separate ways. No hard feelings.

Not that it isn't still like that. I mean, either one of us can grab the safety chute and hit the bomb-bay door any time it's not right. Right?

I could have taken off this morning after Jody read something I wrote and said, "Eh." Her very word, 'eh,' which I took to mean 'not so good,' or just plain 'bad.'

I was out the door. Gone to where the good doggies go. North to Alaska. Back to the Kibbutz. To the Green Mountains of Vermont. I stalked out of our bedroom and defiantly re-read my masterpiece. Then I heard myself say it. "Eh." The very same sound Jody had uttered escaped my lips. It's funny how, after twenty-five years, you begin to talk like each other.

I figured that, just for being a good critic and saving me the embarrassment of publishing an 'eh,' Jody deserved another chance. It was still early in the day. Plenty of time to pack up my troubles in my old kit bag and take the high road to Loch Lomond if she didn't measure up.

Some folks dropped by the house and sat with me in the living room. I was in the middle of telling a story when they interrupted and said the house gave off a warm feeling and what a nice job I'd done decorating.

Decorating? I didn't decorate it. Heck, I didn't even want to buy the place. A hundred-and-something-year-old house? What kind of fool buys a hundred-and-something-year-old house? I told my friends about the day I came home and found Jody, sledge hammer and chisel in hand, standing amid the rubble of demolition. How I remember those days. I'd leave for work in the morning, never knowing which room would be the kitchen when I returned at night. All I wanted was to sleep in the same bedroom two nights in a row. For me, true happiness was finding the water hooked up in the bathroom so I could take a shower. I craved stability; Jody wanted a new Sawsall with extra blades. When I came downstairs after my shower that day, Jody had uncovered a beautiful brick chimney hidden inside the wall.

My visitors left. I never got to finish the story. I couldn't even remember what I'd been talking about and then I looked over at the exposed brick chimney and thought about the changes that have taken place in our house. None of them could have happened without Jody.

Yeah, but what about the plates? Well, that's true. There's been a spell—twenty-four years or more out of the twenty-five—when Jody's been hanging and rehanging dishes all over the walls of our house. I had a nightmare that one day she'd announce all dinners will be eaten standing up. This week's plate color is country red, which at first— yesterday—I didn't like as well as last week's China blue or the week before's French-country yellow. But, you know, I think she got it exactly right this time. And the whole place ties together like... like... home. You know?

It always seems to work like that. Jody does something and my first reaction is to resist the change. Then the miracle happens. When I look again, I'm astounded to discover she's done it just right. I think she puts a spell on me.

Well, except for the mistake. If ever there was reason to split the pea, the mistake was it. Jody hauled me off to a furniture warehouse sale to meet the mistake. It was a beautiful, floral, ninety-inch-long sofa. She pointed at it. "Voilà."

"Voilà what?" I said.

"For the den."

As a rule, I don't get involved in furniture and fixtures. Except, that is, when Jody forces me to lug something from one side of a room to the other and then back again. But I thought it right to point out that this sofa, which was indeed beautiful, was too long for the room for which it was intended and didn't match any of the colors therein. Jody showed me the price tag. Absolutely a bargain. No question. If it weren't too long and the wrong color.

Like a shot, we were back home grabbing samples of wall paper and fabric. Back in the store, the sofa got a draping and I got a "See?" But I didn't see. The color was still off. That afternoon, truckers delivered the sofa to our den. We had a little trouble squeezing by it to get through the room and, although its colors didn't pick up any of the colors in the room, I thought it absolutely eclectic in an eclectic sort of way. To my mind, it had been confirmed again. I was married to a decorating genius.

I have to tell you, that night as I looked around my den, I was one happy guy with our bargain sofa that clashed with perfect élan with everything else in the room. But I detected dark brooding behind Jody's beautiful eyes. The next day, a crew rigged the sofa, now known as 'the mistake,' up to the second-story porch and into our bedroom. A week passed and Jody decorated the den to her satisfaction. I like it, too. But the mistake still lives in our bedroom.

I could leave now. Pick up my life where it was twenty-five years ago. I could do that. The rules are still on. Out the door like a shot. Bing, bang, boom. The Peace Corps in Guatemala. Raise Nubian Goats with a Bedouin tribe. I could do that. You bet.

So, I'm sitting here thinking about what I'll do when it's time to close out this phase of my life. And going over all the great possibilities for a kid like me and Jody's calling from the other room. She wants my opinion on this stenciling project she's doing in our bedroom. When she started, I hated stenciling, but now...

Jody and I are like two hands playing a piano. We don't always hit the same notes, but somehow we get enough melody and harmony to make some pretty nice music.

I think of prospecting for gold in the Klondike and I hear myself say, "Eh." Why would I do that and miss all the fun around here? I still have time. I only hope Jody doesn't decide to bail out first. Then I'd be stuck with the mistake in the bedroom.

A silly millimeter longer

(1993)

In a world gone mad with whizzing projectiles on Moscow streets, ex-skeletal Somalis shooting American kids bent on assuring stable food delivery to remedy their nation's starvation, in a world spinning with revolution and crazy news, I'm measuring the refrigerator. I was seated by the kitchen table at 10 pm with my son, Zev, trying to unravel the mysteries of metric measurement and eighth-grade homework.

I'm an inches-and-foot man myself. My motto: Give metrics an inch, they'll take the yard. Without the bushel and the peck, how can one gauge love? Yet, there I was, armed with a foot-long ruler, a yardstick, a 25-foot aluminum tape measure, and Webster's Dictionary, helping my son understand our refrigerator in millimeters, centimeters, and meter-meters.

There are some lessons in life one is destined never to learn. For me it has been to bring the right tool to the project. I once spent a weekend replacing a four-foot section of house-sill with only a keyhole saw for a cutting utensil. I've no doubt that one of my ancestors looked at some Pharaoh's drawing and said, "Sure we can build a pointy building like that but, without a crane or a jack-hammer, it may take us a while." A thousand years later and—voilà—pyramids.

Zev, provider of our evening's calibrating equipment, is following in the family footsteps. When he tore open the package marked 'metric rule,' he learned the first rule of metrics in America—Americans don't know liters from litter. The calibrations on the ruler were of an inches-segmented foot.

Using Webster's, we looked up *centimeter*—one-hundredth of a meter; and *millimeter*—one-thousandth of a meter; and on to the post-prefixal-root itself, *meter*, where we were directed to the conversion table on page such-and-such.

A millimeter, it turns out, is the equivalent of .03937 inches, give or take some infinitesimal amount, rendering it an inconsequential measurement for Americans looking for the big picture.

I pressed ahead through calculation and manipulation and feeble attempts at explanation to my getting-mighty-sleepy Zev. As we fumbled along, I recalled the last time I'd actually used metric measurement.

I was in Beersheva buying veal cutlets in a butcher shop with my friend, Annette, when the butcher said, "It's a little over a kilo, is that okay?" Annette said it was fine and the butcher wrapped it up. They were great veal cutlets.

Annette now lives in Minnesota.

With only a single time zone separating us, the eleven o'clock hour didn't seem too late to call her with a scientific inquiry. Annette's husband, Avi, answered the phone. Avi is a professor of mechanical engineering at the University of Minnesota. I related our metric dilemma and the story of the veal and asked him to hold while I shuttled the droopy-eyed Zev off to bed.

When I returned to the phone, Avi asked if my calculator had a metric conversion function. It didn't. Then he asked if I had a program where I could plug the numbers into the computer. I don't. So we settled down to the intricate elucidation of metric conversions, by voice, over the phone.

I was scribbling as fast as I could, lost in numbers and decimal places, thinking what a genius that butcher had been to get us that meat so quickly. I said so out loud.

Avi stopped explicating and asked me to repeat the homework assignment. It was to measure some common household items and write the results in metric measurements.

The professor observed that it would be pretty simple to take the measurements with a metric ruler—a ruler having the metric scale on it. I confessed there was none in the house and that was the reason I'd called.

A post-midnight ride to an all-night everything store and $3.59 bought me a 30-centimeter, injection-molded, plastic ruler with an alphabet stencil carved in the center.

Jody asked what time it was as I climbed into bed. I looked at the clock—5:30 am.

As my head hit the pillow, the radio came on with news of the world. Trouble in Moscow. Trouble in Somalia. Trouble here. Trouble there. Somewhere in my subconscious, I made the connection that most of the world's troubles happen in the metric countries. Well, it's no wonder.

Nightmare on Main Street
(1994)

Jody tossed in her sleep again. She was dreaming. I knew what she was dreaming about. When you've been married as long as we have, even the tossing-and-turning of a dream speaks volumes.

Jody was dreaming of Miss Quinn's house. You know the one. On South Main Street. White clapboard, green roof. Gazeboed front porch, left; round turret room, right. Yes, that one. Victoria-Victorianus. Jody was dreaming that she was born to live in that very house.

Jody's dream has become my nightmare.

Let me put this in perspective. Jody will take a rain check on the long longed-for dog in exchange for buying the Quinn house. That's serious.

It's not that I don't like Miss Quinn's house. I do. I love it. It's an incredible house. Easily the house I like second-best in Sharon. Trouble is, I already occupy the house I like first-best.

I have long feared that someday the Quinn house would be put up for sale. I could see it looming after the first of the two elderly Miss Quinn sisters died some years ago. But even when the inevitable comes to pass, one still cries out the obligatory, "Why now?" As if there could be a proper 'now.'

I never met the late Miss Quinns although, over the years, like many in Sharon, I had passing glimpses of bonneted sisters leading a procession of slow-moving traffic along Main Street in their old, black Cadillac. This vision is another of the perks of having lived nearly half a century in our small hamlet where the land sits closer to heaven than at any other spot between Boston and points south and west.

When I learned the last of the Miss Quinns was ill, I prayed for her speedy recovery. Oh, how I prayed Miss Quinn would live forever. Sadly, my prayers went for naught and the gentle lady died in her one-hundred-and-second year. Even mortgage rates dipped to a twenty-year low to mourn her passing. As Chester A. Riley used to say, "What a revoltin' development this is."

That's when the dreams began.

Ever since she was a little girl, Jody loved watching the Quinn sisters pass on review in their travels through town. She loved their hats. She loved the cut of their clothes, the lace, the velvet, the silks and satins. She loved the fox, mink, and beaver stoles that draped their shoulders. My Jody is no mere admirer of Victoriana. She is Victoria reincarnated. If Herself, the Old Queen, had met my Jody, QV-1 would have bowed to Jody's superior Victorian-ness. So when Jody passes Miss Quinn's house, she can't help but stop to wander the yard and touch the gingerbread gazebo, to run her eyes over the nooks and crannies and take in every detail of the old house and its eccentric appointments. Jody can't help it because, in truth, Jody is returning home.

There are some who say I must sacrifice the home Jody and I have lived in for twenty-two years to reunite her with her era. They say we should sit out our days under the pineapple-top gazebo on a love-seat swing, gossamer white-lace curtains answering the summer breezes, Jody waving to the firefighters across the way as they hook their hooks, ladder their ladders, and dash to and from their fiery labors. My Jody, dressed in her summer whites, would offer cool refreshment—a choice of pink or yellow lemonades—to the brave boys and girls of the Sharon Brigade.

In this idyllic vision, humming birds sing in the trumpet vines, tame wisteria resolutely refuse to choke the drain pipes, and mosquitoes buzz in registers far above the range of human hearing and bite only in self defense. The rhythmic music of clopping hooves against cobblestone sets the pace for our heartbeats. Gosh! Wake up Jody. It's only a dream and you're hogging all the covers.

Pretty Boy Floyd, Zen master
(1995)

All his life Pretty Boy Floyd knew that he was born on the very-very spot where the Earth curves to form its sphere. He could feel the curve through the pads of his feet when he walked. He sensed the planet's spin when he fanned his whiskers and he made adjustments for it when he jumped from the roof to the window box and climbed to the top of the highest maple trees. He moved in harmony with the Earth as if guided by an internal gyroscope that kept him in perfect balance with everything around him.

Floyd's mother, Oreo, died within days of his birth and Floyd was raised by Feeder, Jody, Tamara, and Zev who, along with his litter-mate, Fluffy, and the grumpy old cat, Gypsie, made up his immediate family. In his travels, Floyd made other special friends, too—Kim and Lynn Pincus, who live in a house on the other side of the woods that Floyd discovered in his wanderings between North Main and Pleasant Streets.

Early in his life, Floyd understood that he had magical powers. He had the power to make people happy and he took that responsibility very seriously.

Some say that Pretty Boy Floyd was a Zen master, descended from a line of Zen masters. Certainly, some of Floyd's ancestors originated in Siam. That's how he inherited his distinctive fawn-and-brown coloring and his blue eyes. When people looked at Floyd, they had to smile. His round, brown head resembled a lovable panda bear's. And when he sat up after a nap, his torso sank into a banjo shape, like that of Winston Churchill. But something else in Floyd's demeanor—something in his carriage, something in the way he drew himself up to sit statue still—

reminded the observer of ancient cat-gods pictured in hieroglyphics found in the pyramids where Asia and Africa meet. Floyd had a look that suggested that he was inheritor of an ancient knowledge.

Floyd understood that people needed to touch him and, through him, to take on the calm of being in harmony with the Earth.

Floyd lay on his back on the sofa under a sunny south window with his paws spread to the four points of the compass and his body arched to conform to the contours of the planet. He was doing his regular noontime meditation, revisiting his morning's activities.

During the night, he had climbed into bed with Jody and Feeder. Floyd liked to sleep under the covers tucked tight against Jody's body. When Jody rolled in her sleep, Floyd rolled with her, sometimes balancing himself on his back while hanging over the edge of the bed. But Floyd slept soundly in any position as long as he felt the heat from Jody beside him.

In the pre-dawn, Floyd woke and slipped out of bed. His litter-mate, Fluffy, was half asleep in the wicker chair. She rocked it—thu-thump—to let him know she wasn't ready to get up. Floyd went down the hall and pushed open the door to Zev's room. Zev wasn't there. Floyd checked in Tamara's room. She was gone, too. They were both away at school. Floyd missed them. After Floyd's mother died, they had helped Jody and Feeder keep his litter alive, bottle-feeding the infant kittens formula and taking care of their every need.

Floyd looked in on the grumpy, 23-year-old cat, Gypsie, who was snoring in her sleep, wedged in behind a closet door. When he finished his rounds, he arched his back and dug his paws into the carpet. The time had come to start his day outside the house. He climbed onto Feeder's chest and nudged him with his paws. When Feeder didn't respond, Floyd called into his ear. Feeder mumbled but he sat up and opened the window. Floyd slipped outside and left the house over the rooftop.

Floyd headed through the woods to the Pincus house and sat in the window box until he saw movement inside. Doctor Pincus opened the door to collect his morning paper and Floyd dashed in. Barbara Pincus smiled when he entered the kitchen. "Hello, Pretty Boy," she said. Floyd hopped into her lap and nestled there while she stroked him. After a while, he sat up and looked into Barbara's eyes. "You're right, Pretty Boy," she said. "It's time to get the girls up for school."

Floyd raced up the stairs and sprang onto five-year-old Kim's bed. He flopped down next to her and sang a wake-up song. She opened her eyes and pulled him to her. "Good morning, Pretty Boy," she said, and wrapped the cat in her arms. Floyd loved being hugged by his friend. He could feel how happy it made Kim and that made him happy, too.

Barbara called upstairs to the girls.

Floyd went to Lynn's bed and watched her in her sleep. She held her special blanket next to her. He jumped up and flopped down on the blanket. He called her to wake up. When she saw him, she wrapped him in the blanket like a doll and they talked to each other the way three-year-old girls and best friends do.

Barbara watched the girls come down the stairs. She saw Floyd hanging limp, draped upside down over Lynn's arms. His head bobbed as the three-year-old struggled to carry the well-fed cat down the stairs. Barbara was about to object, but the silly expression on Floyd's face told her he loved being in her daughter's arms even if it meant traveling on his back, upside down, hanging like a fur piece.

After the girls were off to kindergarten and preschool, Floyd headed through the woods to check on the neighborhood bird feeders. Birds are so interesting, he thought as he lay on his back and watched the sparrows dart back and forth around one of the feeders in his territory. Mentally, he practiced the motions necessary to snag one from the air, but he was a lover, not a hunter. Besides, the Earth was in motion and the rumble in his stomach said it was time to eat real food and have a nap.

When Floyd arrived home, Feeder was in the kitchen burning toast. Floyd rubbed his body against Feeder's leg. If permitted, Feeder would ignore him until the toast was done. But Floyd was hungry and wanted to eat. He flopped onto his back and grabbed Feeder's foot in his paws. If Feeder thought he could ignore him, well Floyd would just hang on until Feeder took notice. When Feeder moved, he found himself dragging the Siamese cat. "Okay Floyd," said Feeder. He opened a large can of cat food and emptied it into Floyd's bowl. Floyd licked at the juice to test the flavor. Salmon. Okay!

As he ate, Floyd glance over at the couch. The sun was warming the cushions just the way he like them. Soon he would be on his back, meditating, reviewing his morning and planning his afternoon rounds. What a wonderful life, thought Floyd, playing with my humans and keeping them in touch with the curve of the Earth.

The brick wall

(1993)

In this age of electronic highways, cellular phones, e-mail, and CD-ROM, my brain's still cruisin' a sweet-six '56 Chevy convertible, timeless in a time of raging change.

This month the bank Uptown, Our Bank, is replacing its drive-up teller window with a drive-up A.T.M. machine. It seems redundant to say A.T.M. machine, since the 'M' in A.T.M. stands for 'machine'—as the machine stands in the place of a human being—as opposed to 'M is for the many things she's done for me....'

But, in the Age of Acronym, redundancy is S.O.P. The British use the word 'redundant' to describe a person fired from a job, so it seems fair to say one confronts redundancy at A.T.M. machines.

It probably was not a heartless efficiency-freak who designed A.T.M. I think it was someone who remembered asking his mom for money to go bowling. Sometimes she gave it to him, and sometimes it was like talking to a brick wall.

When actual people peopled the drive-up glass, I was reminded of the fortune-dispensing machines found in penny arcades. A quarter in the slot and a card would drop out with my fortune printed on it. At the A.T.M., I insert my Our Bank card in the slot and that machine dispenses my fortune, too, paltry as it may be, and assuming I've P.I.N.-coded correctly. I love secret passwords, so the Personal Identification Number, which in my case is a personal identification word, would be okay if only I could remember it when I need it—when I'm talking to the wall, not just in the bath tub.

I may not know who to blame A.T.M. on, but this obsession with interchangeable words and numerals started with AT&T. First they changed SUnset-4 to 784. Then, in a blaze of numerology, we exchanged HAncocks and GEnevas and, for you ex-New Yorkers, MUrray Hills, for numerals. Digits were here to stay. At least, that's what I believed.

With the installation of the drive-up redundancy, I decided to complain to the bank. It took me over a minute to figure out the right combination of numbers and letters to dial 1-800-OUR-BANK. Then they served me up their menu.

"Thank you for calling the 24-hour Our Bank Line. Now, banking is easier than ever with an Our Bank catalogue. To request your free copy—press ONE. To open a new checking account by phone or to learn more about Our Bank value packages—press TWO. To apply for a consumer loan, credit card, or line of credit—press THREE...."

I was holding for the message that would say, "If you hate A.T.M.— press the hypotenuse of a right triangle where line A – B is 6, and B – C is 9."

Even without the message, I wanted to shoot the messenger. Defiantly, I pressed THREE.

"Please hold," the voice said and muzak came on the line. I was just getting into a groovy, generic tune when a recorded voice interrupted, "Introducing mutual funds at Our Bank...," providing me with enough information on mutual funds to qualify as a doctoral candidate in business administration.

"Mutual funds are not FDIC insured...." Zippy generic tune returns.

After defending my dissertation, I hung up and called the telephone company. 1-800-DIAL-ATT. Remember, these are the same folks that did-in the beautiful SUnsets of my youth.

"Thank you for calling the AT&T customer service and support organization. Our office is presently closed. Please return your call during our normal business hours, which are Monday through Friday, 8 am to 5 pm. Again, thank you for calling AT&T."

It's lonely living drive-up and touch-tone. People don't have time for human contact. Today was typical. The only real people I've spoken to are Burger-Kid at Mickey D's, Chicken-Nuggeteer at KFC, and Donut-Dude at the self-service Exxon. Marketing has turned life upside-down. Out of the car for self-service gas, back in the car for drive-thru donuts.

In such an impersonal time, I suppose it was only practical for that enterprising mark-e-teer in Georgia to institute Drive-Bye wake services. The deceased is enclosed in a glass window like a pre-A.T.M. drive-up teller. Mourners drive by to pay their final respects.

The next logical step will be combining drive-by-funeral-services and fast-food. You'll order 'Wake n' Shake' on your car phone by dialing 1-800 DIE-FOOD.

"If you are calling from a touch-tone phone, please press ONE now... Beep....

"Thank you for calling Wake n' Shake. All of our menus are currently activated. We will take your call in the order it was received. Thank you for your patience. Please enjoy our complimentary sermon-on-hold.

"We pass through this world with great alacrity. Perhaps we should slow down and savor our time together. If you want to order the plain pine box, non-denominational clergy, and chocolate shake—press ONE. If we can assist you with your bank balance—press TWO...."

This above all
(1995)

Next week my daughter, Tamara, will begin law school in New York City. Like Polonius to Laertes, I have a lot of advice for Tamara. And, like Polonius, I'm sure that after she's gone, I'll feel an awful stabbing in my gut.

When I think of New York, I think—termites. Not that the city is infested with termites, it's just that I've always visualized the metropolis as a gigantic termite mound with a frenetic population scurrying about its pheromone-guided activities. With one-and-a-half times the population of Sharon working in a single stalagmite of the Twin Towers complex, New York may well be an intermediate stop in human evolution toward hive society. And that's just the tip of Manhattan.

Manhattan is one of the five boroughs that make up New York City. The word 'borough' is a homophonic variant of the word 'burrow' permuted by a poor speller during the volatile Middle English period. Burrows are holes made in or under the ground for habitation. That's New York.

And then, there are New Yorkers. For half-a-dozen years, I spent three-days-a-week living and working among them. I don't blame New Yorkers for being the way they are. I'd be that way too if I had to phone-up, stand on line, drink egg creams and malteds, eat chop meat, and go to every opening, museum, concert, show, club, and restaurant that finds space to squeeze in on that little island. All in a city where Standard English, when spoken at all, is a third language.

New York is a cultural center without a cultural center. The candy stores serve coffee in blue paper cups with scenes of ancient Greece captioned in ancient Greek. In New York, non-existent nationalities open traditional national restaurants. Looking for the latest in Aztec-Uzbek cuisine? There's a little place in SoHo.

"Yeah, ate there. Saw it. Did it. Loved it. You stood on line for tickets? I hope you didn't pay full price. No, my mother's friend's sister's friend.... Boy, he's no spring chicken. Definitely a rug. You'd think with his money, at least Hair Club, or plugs. And around the eyes. I couldn't look. Sent him a note backstage, said, 'Loved the show, take a tuck. Here's the name of my plastic guy. Mention my name, he'll take care of you.' "

When not being the most generous folks on the planet, New Yorkers are angry. I've walked among them. They scowl. Not at one another. That could be fatal. Anyway, they don't have time to look sideways. Too much to do. They walk straight ahead and scowl straight ahead. They look neither right nor left and, especially, not at other people on the same sidewalk. As they walk, cars try to kill them, predators try to mug them. To survive the daily migration to work and home again is a rite-of-passage. Not all survive the cull.

Every New Yorker is a passionate fundamentalist for some cause or other who, when pushed, will kill for that belief, be it religion, sexual orientation, tolerance, non-violence, race, ideology, politics, nationality, civil liberties, anti-smoking, abortion, choice, save the seals, kill the seals, eat the seals, or Easter seals.

New York is the commerce center of the world and only tourists pay retail. That pattern was established when the Indians dumped Manhattan, land they didn't own, on unsuspecting whites for $24 in real beads.

New York is a city made up of single women and married men each working hard to swap status.

With all that goes on around them, one would think that nothing could faze a New Yorker. That's not true. One day, from my 34th-floor office in the garment center, we heard the sounds of more sirens than usual from the street below. We were in the middle of market week, a time when buyers from all across America come to the New York showrooms to order merchandise for their stores. My sales manager looked down to the street to see what was happening. He stepped back from the window shaking his head in shock and disbelief. A man had jumped to his death from an adjacent building. "Ilan," the manager said, "Why? Why would he do that? It's only Wednesday. There are two full days left in the market." That's optimism.

So, Tamara, as Polonius said, "The time invites you; go." Study hard, play hard, take advantage of the best New York has to offer. And if you get a chance, phone us up sometime.

Home alone, too

(1995)

The kids have gone, Zev to school in Connecticut, Tamara in New York. The other evening, on our first night at home since the kids left, Jody and I made dinner. We work well together in the kitchen. I prepared a zuppa di mare over linguine with red sauce. Jody set the table and went to our wine cellar and chose an Italian red. She uncorked and decanted the wine and she set out a basket of garlic bread and bread sticks. We raised our wine glasses in salute as we do every night, only this time, the 'ting' of the crystal rang soft and mournful. It seemed to signal the start of a new round, or the end of an old one.

The zuppa was delicate, the linguine wound to perfection on our silver forks. The Chianti Riserva accented the flavors of choice sea delicacies. The flame from the long, white tapers cast our flickering shadows onto the kitchen wall. Two empty chairs occupied the spaces between us at the round dining table.

"I miss them," Jody said.

"I'll miss them, too."

Jody sipped her wine then bit into a breadstick. We ate slowly, wordlessly. The only sounds the tinkling of silverware on china and the rustling of cloth napkins.

After dinner, Jody brought the coffee tray into the den. I put Mozart's Piano Concerto No. 21 in C Major on the CD player. We sat across from each other and stirred tiny cubes of sugar into our coffee with demitasse spoons. Our eyes met. I felt my heart pound as I looked at my wife, lover, and friend. The aroma of hazelnut blended with the strains of Mozart in the flickering candlelight.

"What are we going to do?" Jody said.

"On our first date?"

"It does feel like that," she said. "No, with the rest of our lives." She placed a ricotta cannoli on a dessert plate and handed it to me. She'd chosen a thin slice of rum cake for herself.

"I guess we can relax," I said. I licked sweet cheese from the tip of the cannoli. "Be ourselves again."

"But, who are we? Who were we?"

It was a fair question. After twenty-five child-rearing years out of our twenty-six year marriage, did we still have an identity together, alone, without children? Could we stand-down from parental vigilance like post-cold-war armies, or would we be lost without a defined mission? Should we hang the vacated dinner chairs on the wall the way Shakers do, or would the empty space of missing children always be between us? "Did you see the Uptown store is stocking wild goose paté?" I asked.

"I had some," Jody said. "It's very nice. But, you're ducking."

I was ducking, I admitted. "I don't think we've changed all that much," I said. "We're just two kids—hippies, really—with the same simple tastes and desires we had 30 years ago. Would you like a touch of Amaretto to warm the hazelnut?"

"Thank you, no," she said. She lifted her laptop from the floor beside the chaise and placed it across her knees. "I think we should each list the goals and activities we want to accomplish in the years ahead. Then we can run a match for intersecting areas of interest."

"Hold on," I said, and loaded the encyclopedia CD into my Macintosh. The disk whirred and booted. "You know, we could spend an hour or so each evening reading the encyclopedia. Look, the first entry in 'A' is Aachen, a city in northwestern Germany. Charlemagne's northern capital and the center of Carolingian civilization. Wow! Did you know Aardvarks are shy and nocturnal? I'm like that myself."

"Skip to the end," Jody said. She always likes to read the last page of a book first.

I moved the cursor down to the last entry under 'Z.' Zygote, the product formed when two haploids—cells containing half the normal compliment of chromosomes, like a sperm or an egg—combine to produce a cell with a full compliment of chromosomes.

I stopped reading. "Say, that sounds like us. Two newly formed and lonely haploids trying to become a full-fledged zygote." We searched deep into each other's eyes.

"I think I'll have that Amaretto now," she said.

"Make mine a double."

All about the birds and the bees
(1996)

Jody and I have been sitting on the couch in our bedroom a lot lately. We've been holding hands. We've developed an obsession with the birds and the bees. I'll admit that at age fifty, we may be a little late in this regard but, over the years, we've learned to accept things in life as they present themselves, and there's no other way to describe it—we're obsessed.

How obsessed? Well, obsessed enough for me to sublimate my basic rational thought processes and go with this fixation.

Perhaps the explanation is that spring has sprung, and a man's fancy naturally turns to...well, you know where men's fancies turn to in spring. To birds and bees.

Ah, spring. Have you ever stopped to smell the wisteria that hang in bunches like pale, purple grapes against a background of leafy green? Have you ever followed the vine as it merrily threads its way along the trellis and wraps around to weave through the awnings and under the shingles until it mangles the gutters and downspouts and rips the screens and pops the siding off the house? I have.

One morning, about a month ago, I stepped out to my bedroom porch. Brisk spring air filled my lungs. I looked out over my domain. Calmly, I began to inventory the destruction wisteria had wreaked on my roof-water evacuation system—my gutters and spouts. My thoughts ran to pruning shears—massive, sharp pruning shears—to accomplish the massive, sharp job I had in mind.

And then I saw it. Wedged between the screen and the awning. A small collection of grass and twigs. A bird had begun a nest in a fork of the hated wisteria vine. The plan I had just formulated was to slash, hack, and rip this relentless vine from my house and I knew the kindest gesture I could make toward the nest builder was to stop this effort before it advanced too far. The builder would have time to start over in, say, one of the giant maple trees that dominate my yard.

Jody, always the free-spirited dreamer, holds wisteria dearer than downspouts, so my plan had included stealth and speed. I would attack the vine when Jody was away from home. She would return to a fait accompli and I would face the music to the sound of unimpeded water flow.

A few days later, opportunity presented itself. Jody was out of the house and I was home alone. The time was ripe. I dashed to the porch to judge the best angle of attack. A slash here. A slash there. I could imagine the feel of the machete in my hand. I threw my head back and laughed. Hah! From the corner of my eye, I caught the flash of two birds flushed from under the awning. Oh! No! The nest was finished.

Back in the bedroom, I dragged the couch closer to the glass doors of the porch. From this vantage point, I watched the birds return. The little brown one sat on the nest. Her mate with the red-tufted head settled himself into a twist of the wisteria close by her side.

I called the Moose Hill Sanctuary. What did my birds look like? Birds. Smallish birds. Not cardinals or robins. Not hummingbirds or blue jays or vultures. Small birds in the wisteria vine that I'm planning to hack, slash, and burn. Perhaps you have wrens, was the suggestion. Wrens and trouble, I thought.

Off to the library and *Peterson's Field Guide*. Male and female wrens look alike. My interlopers were different. Definitely not wrens. Back on the couch, I scrutinized the pair and called Moose Hill again. What's their song? I didn't know—R&B? Country-and-Western? Rock-a-billy? Kinglets, they said. I watched and listened and ran back to the library. Kinglets looked about right. Not a perfect match, but close.

I hauled the stepladder to the porch and climbed up to take pictures when Uncle John Colaneri called. Finches, he said. The male is reddish? House finches. One-hour photos and a trip to the library confirmed Uncle John's call. Finches.

Back on the couch, I noticed that the female looked a lot rounder than the male. Pregnant? Was Molly Finch pregnant? She was sitting on the nest when Atticus flew in and put food in her beak. Wow. Had I been that attentive to Jody when she was expecting?

The next day, when the Finches were out, I pulled the ladder over to the nest and looked inside. I counted three blue-green, pastel eggs. That night it snowed and for a week the weather was cold and raw. Jody and I paced the bedroom floor. She wanted to put an electric blanket around the nest, but we thought better of it.

After about ten days, the weather warmed up again. Molly was just returning to the nest when I looked out. A tiny beak stuck up in the air from the nest and Molly pushed something into it from her own beak. Jody and I took up a vigil on the bedroom couch. One tiny beak was all we saw. Two days later and we had three. Molly and Atticus took turns feeding the tiny bits of fluff. I moved a video camera onto the porch and set up a light. A few hours later, I retrieved the tape.

When the tape started, Molly and Atticus were out of the nest. Inside, everything was churning. Now and then, an open beak would pop up. Whenever Molly or Atticus landed, all the mouths strained wide open and each, in turn, got some food. Truman, Jem, and Scout's gaping beaks were bigger than the rest of their fuzzy heads. This was a ravenous crew. Something caught my eye. I backed up the tape to get a closer look. Not three sets of open beaks, but four. In the back of the nest, in the shadows, another scrawny-headed fuzz ball was fighting to snag a share of a meal. I named him Boo and called Jody at work to report his appearance.

How will things go for the Finches? Well, I can't say. It can be a tough world out there for babies. I'm glad they helped Jody and me discover the birds and bees. What bees? Oh, they're in the azaleas. But that's another story.

And this story doesn't finish until the fall, when I whack the wisteria

By the silvery moon
(1996)

Last Wednesday, at our usual morning conference, Jody slipped her arms around me. "What do you want to do on Saturday night?" she said.

"We have the bonfire at the lake."

"Are you taking me for granted?"

"I never take you for granted. Seems to me you like bonfires."

"On our anniversary, you think we should go to the lake for a bonfire?"

"And the Fire Department barbecue," I quickly added.

"How many years have we been married?"

I should have seen it coming, a pop-quiz. I tried my standard answer. "We've been together since kindergarten."

"Not this time."

"But, we have. Well, not exactly together-together, but together all the same." I divided my forces—quick calculations in my head, the quick-step with my mouth. "I mean we could have been more together in kindergarten, but you liked whatsizname."

"Twenty-seven years," she said.

"I knew that." And I did know it. I just couldn't get the answer out of my mouth quick enough. "There's a carnival in town," I said. "With fire works. And a Ferris Wheel." Jody loves to ride the Ferris Wheel.

On Saturday—our twenty-seventh anniversary—Jody and I went to the lake. We ate hot dogs and hamburgers at the firemen's barbecue. We bought tickets to ride the Ferris Wheel.

The great wheel lifted us high over the fairway. From our gondola, we watched the Zipper clank and twist and the Pharaoh's Revenge swing to the top of its arc and then drop like a rock. On our twenty-seventh anniversary, the wheel lifted us higher than the tops of the pines that separate the High School field from Memorial Beach. And when we were as high as the wheel could take us, it stopped.

I held Jody in my arms. "I can't imagine a nicer place to be," I said. "Happy anniversary, Jody" As our lips touched, a sonic blast slammed against my chest.

The night sky around us exploded in a bombardment of color and sound. Purple, green, silver plumes shot through the air. Color after color flew up to reach us. Jody and I kissed surrounded by shimmering, phosphorus light and the sound of thunderous explosions.

If our scene had been played out in a movie, even I wouldn't have believed it. But being married to Jody for twenty-seven years has taught me to believe in magic.

From the lake, the bonfire hurled billions of sparks into the night sky. They raced toward the full moon and twinkled above us like a bright new galaxy.

The flames darted and danced. Spectators, who had huddled as close as they could to see the fire lit, pushed back as waves of heat surged across Memorial Beach.

The fire burned brighter and brighter, hotter and hotter, and then it peaked and with its decline, the crowd packed up and headed home. Jody said it was time for us to go, too, but I wanted to stay to watch the fire burn down.

Later, walking home, the smell of the bonfire filled my head. The falling leaves reminded me of the shimmering fireworks that lit our magical anniversary kiss. As I walked, I threw my head back and looked at the face in the full moon. I love the way he winks at me.

My phone bill won't balance

(1996)

I've just had a look at the phone bill. We can forget 10 days/ 9 nights in Guadeloupe. We can forget the day trip to Franklin Park Zoo. It's franks-and-beans month again.

Talking on the telephone is an addiction for people like me. It's like gambling or over-eating. Once we have the bug, once the receiver nuzzles our ear and the mouthpiece brushes our lips, nothing short of a 12-step program can yank us free.

With Tamara and Zev both away at school this year, the telephone bills mount up to real money. I flip through page after page, scanning the list of calls: New York, Connecticut, New York, Connecticut, Connecticut, Connecticut. The calls average about 30 or 40 minutes.

New York—123 minutes. I remember that one. Tamara is in law school in New York. "Just called to say hello." By the time hello became good-bye, I'd learned more about civil procedure than a non-lawyer wants to know. The subtext was that my baby wasn't feeling so well and she was happy to have a sympathetic dad to talk to. The bill shows a 30-minute call to the same New York number a few minutes later. That was Jody. Unsatisfied with my report on Tamara's studies and health, Jody dialed in for more information. Did Tamara need a life-saving fix of home-made pot roast? Chicken soup? Or eggplant? Imagine Federal Expressing a cooked pot roast overnight to Manhattan, the pot roast capital of the world?

Oh, look. An hour and 20 minutes to Connecticut. That was the call where Zev put the phone on his bed while he played me variations of 12-bar blues on his guitar. They sounded great. An hour and 20 minutes. We could have cut an album for less money than I spent on that call.

Minneapolis, Minneapolis, Minneapolis. My friend Avi turned 50 last month. I wrote a note to be read at his surprise party. If our side of the phone record ran into the hundreds of minutes, their calls to us must have occasioned a second mortgage on their house.

Dov and Alina live in Florida. Dov was my teacher when I was 15 years old. I'd seen them only once in the past 35 years. Two years ago, I was asked to go to Florida to speak at Dov's 60th-birthday celebration. The reunion was powerful and we've worked to ensure that our important friendship never lapses again.

The longest call on my bill was to a number I didn't recognize. I asked Jody who it was, but she didn't know either. I dialed to see who would answer. It was my bank. The recording offered a menu of services designed to keep me going around in circles forever. I remember the call. After choosing option after option for more than 45 minutes, I finally got the message that the next available operator would take my call. I waited on the line. They played soft music. I fell asleep. When I awoke the following morning, the pre-recorded message murmured in my ear that the next available operator would take my call. I hung up.

I still don't know my bank balance, but it will be a lot lower for the asking.

Rare sightings

(1997)

Tamara's train left New York's Penn Station at 6:45 on Christmas morning and arrived at Route 128 at quarter-to-noon. She carried two bags; the smaller bag contained clothes; the other, much larger and heavier, held her books. In the car on the ride home from the station, her eyelids blinked, then closed. My daughter was asleep.

At home, she dropped the bag of clothes near the front door and dumped the book-bag in the den near the computer. She kissed Jody and climbed the stairs to her room. When Jody knocked on her bedroom door a few minutes later, there was no answer. Tamara was asleep again.

At two o'clock in the morning, Tamara came downstairs. I was watching television. "Hello, Dad," she said. She gave me a kiss and handed me a disk to load into the computer. While I waited for the machine to boot, Tamara spread her books out over every surface in the den. Then she stood behind me, reached over my shoulder and manipulated the mouse through a series of rapid-fire slashes and clicks until her files appeared on the screen exactly the way she liked them.

We went to the kitchen. Her mother had left a pot of chicken soup simmering on the stove. I sat across the table from my daughter as she slowly sipped the soup from a large cup. She made tiny humming sounds as she drank. The hot soup, with carrots and pastina, acted on her the way morning coffee does for some people. With each swallow, she became more alert. She finished a second cup and looked at her watch.

"I have a 72-hour-final," she said. "I have to get started." She kissed me again, then went into the den and closed the door. I went to bed.

Jody woke me in the morning. "Tamara's at the computer. There are open books everywhere," she said. "When I asked her what she wanted for breakfast, she said she wasn't hungry."

"She has things to do."

On and off, for three days and nights, Jody and I looked in on our daughter closeted in the den. We were greeted with, "Hi, Mom," and "Hi, Dad." The click-click-click of the keyboard stopped only when she pulled a book in front of her to look up a reference or a citation.

Jody kept food cooking on the stove, and from time to time, we'd report to each other that we'd found dishes in the sink.

At dawn on Sunday morning, Tamara woke me. "Can you fax from your computer, Dad?"

"Fax to where? It's Sunday." The look I got told me it was time to get out of bed and set up the modem. The computer dialed and screeched and compressed Tamara's words and footnotes and case citations into bits of transmittable data. The file took 20 minutes to send.

As receipt of the last page was confirmed, I could see my baby's body slump. The modem clicked off.

"Goodnight, Dad. I love you," she said. I barely had a chance to respond, then I heard the door to her bedroom close.

For the next two days, neither Jody nor I reported sighting our daughter. Nor did we find a single dish in the sink. On the third day, in the afternoon, Tamara showed up in the kitchen, showered, dressed and ready to start her vacation. She went down to the video store and picked up a bagful of movies. She returned home, popped one into the VCR, and dropped her tiny frame onto the sofa.

During the week that followed, Tamara went to dinner with us twice. She visited friends and took Zev shopping and bought him a CB radio—a late Hanukkah gift. After each foray, as soon as she was back in the house, she popped another movie into the VCR and flopped herself down on the sofa. A friend dropped off a load of *Star Trek: The Next Generation* tapes. Big Mama Fisher made lasagna and eggplant by the pan-full and hand fed her granddaughter in front of the TV as starships whizzed by at warp speed.

At the end of a week, Tamara told us that on the following morning she would head off to Amherst for a visit and, from there, back to New York.

The night before she left, the four of us—Zev, Tamara, Jody, and I—visited friends. On the way home, Jody took a detour down a little-used lane. Around a bend in the road, our headlights caught two deer as they walked across our path. Jody stopped the car and the deer stopped to look at us. They were fawns, born in the spring, the remnants of white spots still visible on their coats.

The Fishers and the fawns stared at each other through the mist of a warm January night. The deer looked toward the woods. Barely a muscle rippled as they bounded up the embankment and were gone.

In the morning, we brought Tamara to the station to get the bus to Amherst. She climbed the stairs into the bus carrying two bags. The smaller bag contained clothes, the other, much larger and heavier, held her books.

Talking to the wall–Anne Frank
(1995)

Last night, the Orpheum Theater in Foxboro opened the play, *The Diary of Anne Frank*. In addition to the stage production, the Orpheum hosted a photo exhibit of Anne's life provided by the Anne Frank Center. Soon after the exhibit was hung, I went to see it.

Some things are best done alone and, for me, viewing the photos of Anne Frank and her family was a solitary event.

The panels are arranged in chronological order, Anne as a baby, then as a child, and a young girl. I came to the famous photo of Anne Frank as a 12-year-old. I studied her eyes, the light and promise of the whole world still before them. Yet they were haunting. I stared into those large, brown eyes and thought of the diary entries she would write in just a few short months. Here were eyes that took in everything around them, the eyes of a writer already sifting through her vision for secrets to be discovered. Eyes ready to record faithfully and honestly. As I looked into Anne's innocent eyes, I was shaken, for I knew the awful truth they would come to see.

In my mind, I couldn't help but follow her vision to places I didn't want to go, to visualize the horrors she would see. "Anne," I wanted to scream out to her. "Anne," I wanted to whisper in warning. "You are going to see truths about human beings that you don't want to know." But how could I say those things to a picture of a girl dead 50 years ago?

Someone entered the gallery and I dropped my gaze to a caption on the photo board. I read slowly to give myself time to return from the place where I'd been. Would it seem strange to find a man of 48 years with tears in his eyes standing in front of a photograph of a girl he'd never met, a girl dead before he was born?

The photographs of Anne stop at age twelve. The exhibit contains other pictures, pages from her diary, photographs of the secret annex where the Frank and Van Daan families hid for two years before they were captured and deported to the camps. There are also pictures of their protectors, non-Jews who risked everything to try to save the eight people under their care, hiding them, feeding them, even trying to entertain them with books and presents.

Today, August 4, is the anniversary of Anne's capture, 51 years ago.

Some time ago, I came to understand that the story of the Holocaust is not well understood when told in millions of murders. Millions were murdered. Each was a person. Each a distinct individual, as you and I are distinct, as our children are individual. Anne Frank was one of the murdered. If we start counting, there was a number two, and a three, and the numbers keep adding up long past incomprehensible.

The 15-year-old Anne Frank died 50 years ago in Bergen-Belsen. Through her writing and her photographs, for us, she will always remain a young girl. She was an honest and gifted writer whose insights and observations seem to flow effortlessly onto the pages of her diary. Through her diary entries, we can imagine her incessant chatter in the Annex; we can feel the clock tick out the long hours she was forced to sit, silent, hiding from the killers; we can feel her loneliness. And we can experience the sensations of Anne's emerging womanhood and her promise unfulfilled.

If we could talk to Anne, what would we tell her of the changes in the world a half century after her death? Knowing her fate, would a country today intervene on her behalf? Could we assure her that the rail line that transported her from Holland to Belsen would be bombed? I'd like to tell her that there are places called safe havens, pockets of safety that moral countries would fight to protect. I would like to say that morality is now recognized as a strategic interest by the world community. I would like to say those things to her. A few years ago, I might have said them. Today, I could not.

Some argue that Anne Frank—that all the victims of the Holocaust—are diminished by comparison to the victims of ethnic cleansing that has been going on in Bosnia. I believe the opposite is true. Anne Frank—all the victims—are murdered over and over again if we did not learn to act.

Magic ice
(1995)

Magic came to town last week.

She rode in on a cloud of mist and embraced everything, from rooftops to roadways, bog grass to beech boughs, in elegant patterns of ice that dazzled the eye and dizzied the senses. Long-time residents swore that never before had the landscape worn a tunic of such delicate majesty. Magic turned the countryside to glass and painted it in shades of light and white. People gathered to watch as twigs and branches transformed to holiday baubles and, like children, they competed to call out the names of colors when jeweled droplets changed from garnet to amethyst, topaz, and sapphire, as the sun played across the sky.

We awoke that first morning inside a palace of spun ice with enough silver and gold hanging from every bough to overflow the coffers of a thousand-thousand kings. Every tree, every fence, every blade of grass added new wonder to the world as breathtaking as any of the other grand wonders and as close to home as our own window view.

The magic ice alighted like a diamond tiara crowning our treetops. It stayed as if there were no place more deserving in the whole world for it to be. It stayed as if we had been granted a gift from the gods. And each morning, when we woke and found the magic still with us, we marveled anew that we remained the world's favored. And in our heightened awareness, we rediscovered all the beauty around us as clean as dawn on the first day.

To walk past a window was a gift. To walk to the railroad station was a delight. To walk along a wooded path was wonderment.

While the magic ice was with us, the mundane became magnificent and the magnificent, majestic.

Children and adults sampled the new, strange fruit of the oak, pine and maple trees with the tips of their tongues to see if the crystalline branches were really sweet rock candy, or warm taffy, or cool ice. And when the testing was done, none could give a satisfactory answer to those questions, for magic ice can bend like soft wax, and it has the taste of sweet grass, and, it feels both warm and cool on the tongue.

Then on Saturday, the sun rose high in the sky, warmer and somehow, if such a thing is possible, sadder than I had seen it before. Like a peacock at full fan, it shone in full spectrum and, as if in a parting kiss, the ice reflected back a display of jewel colors, new birthstones—rebirth stones—unequaled and unseen ever before in all the world.

As if answering the sun's call, a mist rose up from the branches and buds, from the grasslands and birch boughs. A magic mist like the one that rode in on the cloud that brought the magic ice to our town. Like parting lovers, slowly the ice loosened its embrace and slipped to the ground.

The mist rose to the heavens, to reform there, I supposed. And to move on, to take some other town hostage to delight. I don't know. I can't say.

The loss of a lullaby
(1995)

My friend Annette Bar-Cohen sent me a copy of *The Will to Live: Memoirs of a Survivor 1939-1945* by her father, Jack Pavony. I had read it before. The book tells of Jack's life during the Holocaust. This new edition contains a photograph of Jack with his two children and five grandchildren. I re-read the story of Jack's Holocaust experiences and, knowing his family as I do, I was again struck by the courage, durability, and luck that enabled Jack not only to survive the Holocaust but to survive the survival. Recently, I had an experience with another survivor, a grandmother, and glimpsed the demons she still fights. I think the stories go together.

The date was early September, 1939. Jack Pavony, then Yaacov Piwonia, was one month shy of his thirteenth birthday and preparing for the first day of a new school year. That morning, in the skies over Poland, German planes invaded his life and blew it apart. Jack would never again prepare himself for a day in school. The falling bombs blasted the rhythms of his life and launched him on a frenetic journey that lead through ghetto and cattle car to Auschwitz, Matthausen, and finally, liberation and life.

For five years after the bombs set him in motion, each step that he took was taken amid lunacy, lawless barbarism, murder, chaos, and death, punctuated by episodes of selfless humanity from some brave other also caught in the berserk asylums of the 'Final Solution.'

When liberation came and the safety of the American army surrounded him, Jack asked himself, Where is my mother? Where is my father?, though he knew that both had been slaughtered at Auschwitz, his mother ripped from his hands within moments of their arrival, his father selected a few months later by Mengele. The 13-year-old, now 18, woke from a nether world where starvation, beatings, torture, and killing were the norm and where Mengele, selector of death, had stared into his eyes countless times and miraculously passed him by. It was time to reconnect to life.

After liberation, Jack married Bronia and they had a daughter, my friend, Annette. The family came to America. Here their second child, Howard, was born. Then, within a few years, Bronia, who had survived Nazis and Auschwitz, died of cancer.

Jack and his children picked up the pieces of their lives and went on.

On Shabbat, the ninth of February 1986, at 10:30 pm—forty years after his liberation at Matthausen—Jack sat alone in a room with a tape recorder and, for the first time ever, spoke the story of his life between the years 1939 and 1946. He spoke haltingly, and in great pain, as the memories washed over him. He spoke the stories in Yiddish, the language of his experience. He spoke to liberate himself and his children. They translated his words into English and presented them to him in a published book on June 10, 1986, his sixtieth birthday. This week, his daughter, Annette, sent me the expanded edition, the one with the picture of Jack and his five grandchildren.

A few months ago, I filmed a Bat-Mitzvah girl reading from the Torah. As I widened the camera shot, I saw her grandfather, his eyes closed, gently rocking to the melody his granddaughter chanted. Watching the scene through my viewfinder, I found myself humming an old Yiddish lullaby I'd learned as a child. The song describes the warmth of a brick hearth, a pripetchik. In front of the hearth, a rabbi sits teaching a child to pronounce the Hebrew letters he will need to chant the words of the Torah, just as the young Bat-Mitzvah girl was doing. The lullaby describes the warmth of the hearth and the warmth of the love of teaching and learning.

Watching the grandfather swaying as his granddaughter recited, I thought of that hearth and the warmth that ties generations together.

Later, I added the lullaby as background music to the filmed images.

Soon after delivering the tape, I got a call from the girl's father. He said that his whole family had gathered in front of the television with great expectation to watch the video. When the scenes of his daughter and father began, his mother, an Auschwitz survivor, cried out and ran from the room, sobbing uncontrollably. He ran after her and tried to calm her. Through her sobs, she said she had to escape the room when she heard "that Holocaust music" on the tape.

Holocaust music? Oh, no. I could feel the tears well up in my eyes. Certainly not Holocaust music. A lullaby, sung to join generations, certainly not to cause pain.

The man told me that never before, never once in his life, had he seen his mother cry or heard her speak a word of the Holocaust.

When he brought me the tape to redo the music, I showed him a copy of the song. "Look," I said, "it's simply a lullaby. A song parents have sung to their children."

We use the word Holocaust in the singular to encompass the deaths and altered lives of millions. But their experiences are a vast plural, like the universe blown apart, shattered into tens of millions of pieces, different for each individual whose life compounds that word. Every week, I learn more stories of the Holocaust and its survivors. Some are as terrible as the loss of a beautiful lullaby.

The wall that separates a generation

(1994)

My friend, Tom Quin, showed me a newspaper column by James Carroll, author of the novel *Mortal Friends*, a story that begins during the Irish rebellion and speaks to themes of loyalty and betrayal, insurrection, revolution, and the choices that people make. Carroll's newspaper column in last week's *Boston Globe* about Vietnam protest, mirrors those themes.

Carroll writes about a man who, early in the Vietnam War, in 1965, drove to the Pentagon, doused himself with kerosene and burned himself to death right under the window of Secretary of Defense Robert S. McNamara. Carroll's father, an Air Force officer with a Pentagon office down the hall from McNamara's, never spoke about the man who forfeited his life in the parking lot in order to bring attention to the Vietnam War.

Carroll puts forth the premise that, "as a nation, we have yet to find a way to acknowledge the acts of those who opposed the war," and he offers his column to preserve the memory of those who served their country by not going to war.

Tom Quin, who brought me the piece, was a Navy lieutenant during the Vietnam era.

Tom is a very straight-forward man. He will tell you that, during his service in the Navy between 1968 and 1971, he made three cruises to Southeast Asia, each lasting between six and eight months. He was fortunate that, even when operating off the coast of Vietnam, his ship never came under fire. But Tom was every bit a United States Naval officer and, as such, would have taken his ship wherever he was called upon to serve.

Tom and I talked about the options open to our generation during the Vietnam era: college deferments, Canada, duty, enlistment, protest, jail—choices and non-choices for a war that, at first, didn't require our attention at all if we went on to college after high school.

After World War II, the Selective Service System was revamped to spare college students from gunfire. But for those of our generation less well-off, less literate, without direction, caught between deferments, or for those eager to serve and willing to forgo the deferments offered, Vietnam was waiting.

During the Civil War, draftees could buy their way out of service by paying another to go to war in their stead. During Vietnam, the fees were paid to college bursars.

Even after all these years, Vietnam is still a muddled mess of rights and wrongs. The wall in Washington, built to memorialize our dead and bring us together, may be just as symbolic of our generation's divide. The memorial is, after all, a wall.

Thinking back to Carroll's musings about recognizing the contributions of those who opposed the war, might I suggest that a blank panel added to the Vietnam Wall would be appropriate. An empty panel. A clean slate. Without names. As highly polished and reflective as those panels containing the names of the 53,000 dead of my generation. A panel that says, without words, that if not for the massive anti-war effort in the streets, on the campuses, and ultimately in the electoral process, politicians, generals, and intelligence agencies would have kept the list of names escalating, and more and more panels would have been needed to write the names of our war dead.

Perhaps a single blank panel, polished like the others, to mirror-perfect perfection, would afford each person of my generation—whether he fought or not—a chance to stand before the Vietnam divide and look at himself. To see himself reflected side-by-side with the names of our dead and decide for himself if he served the United States of America. So maybe there should be a new kind of memorial where the living who served or didn't, acted, reacted, or were swept along by events, can confront themselves and decide whether they were true to the full spirit of what it means to be an American. A memorial to reflect a generation.

Summer curves

(1993)

Walking along Pond Street, I noticed a ball game in progress at the high school field. I drifted over to the bleachers to watch the game and enjoy the sun.

Sharon had a man on first. A batter stepped up to the plate. The pitcher checked the runner, stepped toward the plate, and released his pitch. His body trailed off the mound to the first base side. The batter squared off and dropped a bunt foul down the third base line.

A spectator told me the score. With a man on first, the pitcher went into his stretch, held the runner with a long look, then stepped toward the plate with his delivery, again finishing off the mound toward first base. The batter attempted another bunt and like the first, it rolled foul.

With the threat of a bunt foreclosed, the third baseman repositioned himself back a few steps. On a two-strike count, it was time to stuff the batter with a fast ball in tight enough to shave his armpits or run a slider in at the knees.

I smiled in anticipation.

The man next to me cupped his hands to his mouth. "Right by him, baby," he yelled to the pitcher. "Right by him."

The pitcher stretched, looked toward first, and threw a fastball in tight. The batter punched it off the handle near his knuckles. The ball dribbled to the pitcher's right catching him off balance with no way to recover. The third baseman charged but the batter beat out the throw.

The spectator cupped his hands and yelled, "Lucky hit. Lucky hit." Then turning to me said, "Lucky hit off a good fastball."

"An easy double-play," I mumbled back absentmindedly, then added that the pitcher needed a good coach. The spectator glared. The pitcher was his son. He'd taught him to pitch.

"No follow-through," I said. "He got caught. Follow-through. Follow through. His fastball will be faster. He won't get caught out of position like that, and you'll save his arm wear and pain."

I think the words 'save' and 'pain' saved my life. While his son pitched, the father moved closer to me on the bench. As if by rote, I explained why his son was so vulnerable to bunts and dangerously exposed to having his head ripped off by a hit smashed back to the mound. But, mostly, I heard a voice from inside me expounding the philosophy and rhythms of pitching, the mantra I'd learned so many years ago from the greatest sports coach ever—Murray Fisher, my dad.

To Big Daddy, pitching was art, a matter of form and physics, form and fluidity, motion and leverage, dance choreography where every movement was practiced to perfection. For his eight-year-old son, a boy with a 60-pound body and a strong arm, who could hit almost any target he chose to throw a rock at, pitching baseballs was an irrelevant imposition on his life—at least it started that way.

Big Daddy was an exacting master, brooking no tolerance for deviation or individuality in the precision of pitching. And he had determined that I would pitch.

I learned to lean in to read a catcher's sign. Then in seamless fluid progression, my arms and legs, my body, learned to rock, rise, twist, arch, and extend in interactive fulcrums and shifting centers of gravity designed to project every pound of my frame and weight into a white round projectile moving through space toward a fixed point. Even as I launched the ball, my body reconfigured its momentum for touchdown, always square to the target and poised to move defensively in any direction.

The total—from lean in to follow through—was a complete dance where every motion and body part assists and compliments all others. There are variations on the dance but the essential parts always remain the same.

As I got older, Big Daddy allowed me to throw breaking pitches.

First came the curve, a sharp-breaking curve that jumped away from a right-handed batter and sank. My fingers started on top of the ball then snapped downward to set the spin that caused the ball to jam the air then break and drop.

But the slider was the ultimate, the most glorious pitch ever devised. I loved its easy roll off the inside of my fingers. Where the curve required a hard snap of the wrist, the slider was the soft touch. What seemed, at first, like the most unnatural rotation possible for a wrist and hand, became my pitch. My motion was perfectly designed to throw it.

Releasing the slider was a matter of practice and precision timing. Unlike the curve, which cost me some effort to throw, the slider was savory dessert, delicious perfection as it slid off my fingers. Thousands of hours of throwing baseballs at a painted target on a concrete wall had patterned my slider from lean-in to follow-through. As it left on its flight, I could feel the rightness of its delivery. To a batter-hunter, crouching, lurking over the plate, straining to smash a fastball or a curve, the slider was the poisonous snake that would lunge at his legs when his senses failed to detect its reverse spin in the air.

The visiting pitcher's dad interrupted my thoughts.

"So, if I understand you correctly, you're saying pitching baseball is Zen."

I thought about it and I had to nod in agreement.

He continued. "And pitching a strike-out would be nirvana?"

"No, strike-outs are only a by-product of good pitching and, like achieving a good life, a matter of properly balanced centers of gravity."

"And nirvana?"

"Nirvana is someplace else."

"How can I teach it to my son," the father asked, "if you won't tell me?"

I closed my eyes. So many years had passed since... I felt a tingle run up my body, down my right arm and into my fingers. "Teach your son," I whispered wistfully, reliving a pitcher's moment in time... "Tell him nirvana lies in the last touch of a perfectly thrown three-and-two-count slider gliding from your hand as your body ends up square to its target, poised and ready to field a hit you know will never come."

From here to eternity
(1995)

I'm a man of property. Not just any property, but property in one of the most expensive subdivision in New England. Property-in-perpetuity, parcel ad infinitum. Yes, I'm an owner in Sharon Memorial Park.

Back in the 1950s, my folks bought a pair of adjoining plots at SMP. A few years later, they added to their holdings with the acquisition of six rectangles situated near the original lots. As of this week, I own those six plots.

Owning perpetual real estate forces me to think about eternal questions. Assuming the usual course of events, my property will one day be owner occupied. That's a lot to think about.

On one level, I like the memorial-park concept: grass, trees, flat markers set in the ground. I can see how the idea of flat markers caught on when they first started using them back in the '50s and '60s. Easy care, low maintenance. Like vinyl siding. On the other hand, I find walking through a cemetery of irregular granite and marble grave stones deliciously unpredictable, as authentically pleasing as the discovery of pink quartz inlaid with purple lettering.

With the invention of the Weed Whacker, loved ones need no longer worry that graveyards will revert to jungle landscapes, like the temple in *Congo*, where lurking creatures feel compelled to make their home.

Fortunately for me, I have a friend who's an expert in gravestones. Tombstone-Bob Seriski works for Davis Monument Company. Tombstone and I were friends in a previous life when we both worked in the garment industry. So, we have some expertise in early demise.

I explained to Bob that, although I own the six parcels in SMP, I'm uncomfortable about the prospect of being buried in them before I'm fully committed. I don't mean I'm afraid of being buried alive—of course, I worry about that possibility—but I'm having trouble choosing memorial parks over monument scapes. Specifically, I'm worried about how few words fit on a 28 x 14-inch bronze plaque.

The typical marker at SMP is inscribed with name, dates of birth and death, and a sentence fragment like, 'Loving husband, son, and father.' That's less information than you're required to provide captors under the Geneva Convention. Bob said that at some memorial parks, people use small letters and write epitaphical poems and such. Over the years, SMP has evolved a certain style. When choosing inscriptions, people look at the other markers in the park and tend to keep to that style.

Of course, with my six plots, I could cluster zone my plaques and, by adding 'cont.' or 'next,' and an arrow, indicate that the reader should move from bronze to bronze. Employing that technique, I could write whole paragraphs including the run-on sentences I incline towards.

Staying with the option of smaller lettering over multi-surfaces offers the possibility for an encapsulated life history or serial epitaph. 1. Colicky from birth to college. 2. Sucker for a hanging curve. 3. Flunked finger painting. 4. Played with his food. 5. Lactose intolerant.

Of course, I would need to use all six of my plots just for me. Poor Jody would have to fend for herself.

For solitary plot holders, epitaphs are more attainable at monument cemeteries.

I particularly like the Baker Street Cemetery in West Roxbury where my grandparents are buried. Many of the stones date back to the 1920s, '30s and '40s and have porcelain photographs of the interree on them. Bob told me that space-age epoxies now prevent vandals from stealing the porcelain off the markers and people are again choosing photos. But, he said, more often they opt for a likeness drawn from a photograph, then etched in color into black granite. Sounds nice.

But, where are cemeteries with CD-ROM and fiber-optic technology? Is there yet an interred-net?

Bob says the day may not be far off when a visitor will go to a gravesite, be it a bronze plaque or rock obelisk, press a button, and see a TV image of the deceased on a screen, speaking a pre-recorded message. Or, messages might be individualized, accessed on-site or by phone through the use of ID codes or phone cards. When purchasing a cemetery plot, the future interree will record answers to a psychological-profile computer questionnaire. The program will generate conversations based on the likes and dislikes of the deceased, as well as the historical relationship to the card holder. Questions, answers, and general discussion will be lip-synced to video images of the deceased. Like Jor-el, the Brando character in Superman. In this way, the deceased will exist forever in a fiber-cyber world. Let there be light.

With all these technologies and choices over the horizon, it's not easy being a man with property. I guess, for now, I'll just sit on my land, think eternal thoughts, and see what develops.

Turn on, tune in, and dial

(1993)

After three years of receiving *Victoria's Secret* catalogs, I still don't know which model is Victoria, but when I called the *Girls' Innermost Secrets Hotline*, within 15 minutes on the phone, I knew everything there was to know about Wendy, Buffy, and Attyla, and I have valuable appointment minutes already scheduled with their friends to tell me even more secrets.

Watching night-owl cable TV has initiated me into a world so much more stimulating than the ho-hum, work-a-day world inhabited by earthlings confined to living on a single time line, out of touch with their previous and future lives, existing in daylight, yet desperately in the dark, lonely, balding, overweight, with bad skin and failing memories.

It was the dean of late-night infomercials and 900-555 numbers, Dr. Robin M. Blynd, who opened my intellect, introducing me to touch-tone friends, timeline travel, and oh, so much more. Here's how it all started:

TV voices: My boyfriend has proposed to me, what should I do?... Were you rich, famous, or Napoleon's pet turtle in a previous life?... Want to unlock the beauty secrets of the Orient?... Need a fuller, more natural-looking head of hair?... Has a sunken chest expanded your waistline?... Dying to know innermost secrets?

Hi. I'm Dr. Robin M. Blynd. Right now you're probably hopping up and down on one leg, screaming, 'Yes, Dr. Robin M. Yes.'

I looked down. It was true. I was pulling on my jammy bottoms, trying to get my second leg in, hopping around the room precariously balancing on one foot.

TV voice continues: The answers to these and thousands of other questions hammering inside your head are as close as Dr. Robin M. Blynd's Boudoir-Phone Hotline—$3.95 per minute. Children under 18 years of age should not call without permission of adult. Adult need not be a relative. The hamburger flipper at a local take-out will do. Offer void if prohibited by law.

I lost my balance and crashed to the floor. These were important questions Mr. TV Voice was posing. Not the usual fare of sex, superficiality, and violence. This was philosophical stuff. I thought I'd better check it out.

I dialed the number flashing on the screen. 900-555-L-E-R-N, and pressed the 'pound-key' to indicate I was interfacing touch-tone. I love modern gadgets, don't you?

Before AT&T could ring up a 15-minute segment, I learned that Dr. Robin M. was author of *The Tofu Solution—A Remedial Guide to Yuppie Sensuality* and *Aerobics, No Sweat*. His *Papier Mache' or Plastic Surgery?—Paste Your Way to a Firmer Future* includes a special section on nose sculpting.

In a second segment, I learned that Dr. Robin M.'s mail-order degree in theology and out-of-body experience (due to a shooting incident with law enforcement) inspired the founding of *The Medium Channel*, as well as authorship of *From Gold Dust to Gold Dust—A Channeler's Handbook to Inter-Life Trusts*, and *Antiques Like New*, wherein Dr. Robin M. teaches tried-and-true techniques for purchasing antiques direct from their original owners in their original time periods.

In the third installment, Dr. Robin M. Blynd revealed a pioneering achievement in networking multiple personalities with themselves through a patented 900-555 e-mail your self yourself service. And for $29.95, you can receive the latest paperback, documenting how Dr. Blynd saved customers hundred of dollars in duplicate book orders by cross-referencing their multiple personalities and adding all their names to a single shipping label.

By our fourth segment, Doc and I were really tight and I was offered the opportunity to franchise my own Dr. Robin M. Blynd official 900-555 number, to work right out of my home and in my favorite time slot, dusk to dawn. I got to choose from a wide list of hotline franchise topics.

TV voice: Hi, I'm Ilan. Join me and the millions of other Americans who have saved thousands of dollars by avoiding expensive psychotherapy. For a mere $3.95 per minute, I or one of my trained assistants will guide you *through Dr. Robin M. Blynd's do-it-yourself analysis. Plus, you'll meet lots of great new friends and own more books than L. Ron Hubbard has in his cupboard. So, why call Michael J.'s sister or Cher, cherie? If you want to learn more about yourself call me at.....*

See, then I put my hotline number there.

There's only one problem. If I'm busy helping all you folks who call my hotline, when will I get to talk to the girls over at *Innermost Secrets*?

Water rights

(1997)

Welcome back to Sharon. If you were off planet for the summer, or in Colorado, you probably missed the big story here these past months, the one about the black hole that's been siphoning our drinking water out of Lake Massapoag. You may say Massapoag water tastes terrible and you wouldn't drink it unless you were beyond parched and I wouldn't argue. I'm just fillin' you in on the news that happened while you were out of town.

I hope you didn't leave your automatic sprinkler system on while you were gone. If you did, you probably found a pile of citations on your stoop and a summons to go to a Selectmen's meeting when you arrived home.

If you can afford to put in an automatic watering system, the fines won't mean much, but you still have to sit through an entire Selectmen's meeting. And you'll have to bring your whole family, including the au pair. Now maybe you're a tough guy, but think about the kids. If, after that, you continue to use the automatic sprinkler, they make you go to a School Committee meeting. A choice of hanging by the neck until dead or attending a Lake Management Committee meeting is next, but nobody ever made it past School Committee.

So, about the lake.

When I first met Lake Massapoag as a young swimmer, there was plenty of water and lots of leeches in there, too. I was a healthy child, probably because of all the medicinal bleeding. Over the years, the leeches disappeared. Now it's the water itself that's going away.

Massapoag is a spring-fed lake. At least, that's what folks think it is because they can only find about two or three small brooks running into it and that's not enough water, they say, to make a big lake like Massapoag. So, the lake experts theorize that it must be spring fed.

Historians too young to know better say the lake was the result of a mining accident. The story goes that, a long time ago, Massapoag was an iron mine and guys were digging and hammering at the ground when suddenly the mine sprung a leak. The story is only a myth, a bubba-meiser grandmother's tale, but some folks believe it's true.

The real story is that this one feller working down there in the mine saw a pheasant. He picked up his flintlock thinking he had a sure shot at dinner on the table and fired at the bird. The musket ball went right through the pheasant and into the ground. Lickety-split, water shot up from the hole. Old Jed Clampert threw down his gun and tried to sop up the water with his handkerchief but the flow was more than a man could handle. A powerful spout slammed into his midsection, pushed him right up out of the mine, down Pond Street, and on into Canton where people say that, as he flew by, his flailing arms and legs built the viaduct and Revere Copperworks before he was dumped into Boston Harbor and was washed far out to sea, as far as Ireland, where his arrival scared all the snakes off that island, but he couldn't do anything about the British.

Now, as of this moment, no one has ever located Clampert's mine, the springs that feed Massapoag, or the black hole that's been stealing our water.

One local academy of amateur semi-knowledgeable self-styled water experts say that Sharon actually sits atop a giant bathtub aqua-fryer or Fry-a-lator or something, and that all the water on Earth bubbles up from inside our borders. Last year, somebody neglected to sacrifice a chicken or a goat and the Great Spirit pulled the drain plug on us and now we won't have good swimming or sprinkling water for seven lean years. They say that, up until now, Sharon could afford to be generous about providing water to our neighbors, Canton, Easton and Foxboro, towns that have little or no indigenous water resources of their own, but from now on, Sharon may have to ration out water to them or stop their flow altogether.

So, here comes the news about the override. One official or semi-official official started talking about the only way to save our water was tanks and I asked him how many water tanks we would need to store up enough water for... He cut me off short and said that he wasn't talking about water tanks, he was talking about a squadron of battle tanks with big guns mounted on them, and Apache helicopters, and conscripting an army to protect our bathtub from the surrounding thirsties, and even if we put all of Sharon's high school kids in uniform, the cost would still be cheaper than sewage fees and that's what's been happening in Sharon.

So, how was your summer?

'tis the season to be malling
(1993)

It's not that I don't understand the concept of 'mall.' I do. A mall is an inside-outside area with shops and corridors, surrounded by acres of asphalt painted over with yellow and white lines, accessible by feeder roads that open onto interstate highways, which have exits only after long intervals, and always end up in places like Jacksonville, Florida.

That I understand.

It's how people—plain human folk—are able to negotiate the complex maneuvers involved in leaving the security of their automobile in one of those parking lots to navigate the hive of merchandise, then to embark on a return expedition to that same car hours later.

That's what I don't understand.

For me, an African safari would be a whole lot simpler. That's why I don't go to malls. That, and the fact that they're out to get me.

Only once a year, during the holiday season, and after much mental fortification, will I risk a trip to a mall for a single compulsory purchase. A present for Jody.

Anticipating my imminent arrival to buy for my wife the pair of woolen bovine hosiery she so yearns to own, spidery mall-managers, those hum-bugging trollers of meaningless merchandise, wait to ensnare me in a web of goods-and-services designed to keep me bound within their maze of corridors forever.

Why?

My magnetism of course.

I possess a wallet full of thin plastic cards with such magnetic allure that no maller can resist me. They prepare their snares by kiosking every inch of interior buy-way with carts hawking velveteen-painted-

Elvises, cowboy-style belt buckles, photo-ops with Santa, hammered jewelry, glass figurines, tie-dye tee shirts, and smoked salamis. The sights, the sounds, the indulgent array of colors, mechanical displays, book titles, fashions, uniforms, cosmetics, greeting cards, video images, blinking lights, twinkling stars, and people by the mall-full entice me to linger and stare and, through these devices, infect me with that malady pandemic to the last decade of the 20th century—insatiable Mallhead.

I fight to resist. But, each item has been strategically positioned to vie for my attention and, worse yet, each stands a good chance to snag a piece of it. A thousand-ring-circus. Sensory overload. Boom. Merchandise comatose. Call out the mall EMTs. Ring me up and out.

I would buy everything. Every last deeley-bopping thing. Could I possibly have touched a Nash Metropolitan in a sweat-suit store? When did sweat suits get their own stores anyway?

I drag my thoughts back to the task at hand, cow socks, and beyond that to car and home. Home and car—just one more time, Lord. It's blue and has a 'Tsongas for President' sticker on the bumper.

I bull my way forward, grab the bovine beauties from the rack, and escape to the corridors, the labyrinthine maze still between me and the safety of blue car and home.

I scramble to an Outlet Store and push past the chocolate-turtle petting zoo. A sign reads, 'If Toy's 'R Us, then who are we?' As I stop to ponder, mall-elves snatch at my wallet. I break free and dive for the teeny-tiny, faded-red exit sign. Bing Crosby in a Santa suit waves me through to the parking lot. Where there's Bing there's Hope.

Now to find my car. Other escapees tumble out after me. Many possess magical key rings that permit communication with automobiles. Thousands of cars respond in a chorus of whirps, chirps, and whistles. "Was that mine or yours?" the lady with blue hair asks. A crowd of respondents look down at their key chains and each presses his personal Ident-if-I in unison. More whirps and chirps. I see desperation in their haggard faces. A man wearing an 'All the way with LBJ' button passes by, his beard sweeping the asphalt. How long have these people been searching?

I'd come to the mall for cow socks for my lovely Jody. Now, I want to go home. I click my heels together. Auntie Em, Auntie Em.

D-Day plus fifty

(1994)

The world was a smaller place once and, among the friends of my childhood, almost everyone's dad had traveled somewhere in it. We have photographs to prove it: pictures of my father in Karachi and Delhi, and flying the 'hump' into Kun-Ming, China. There is a favorite picture of my Uncle Sidney in the South Pacific, leaning against a railing on the Battleship *New York*, and another of the *New York* with a kamikaze plane jutting from her upper deck after it killed eight of the twelve sailors assigned to that station. Uncle Sidney was one of the four lucky ones.

Before the world got to be a bigger place, my dad sailed through the Suez Canal, saw the Taj Mahal, and looked down on the Himalayas. Most of the neighborhood kids' fathers had traveled, too—through Italy, England, France, and North Africa. They'd flown missions over Germany. Some even got to visit ancestral hometowns.

And they saw America. Training at the Great Lakes or Biloxi, Parris Island or Fort Dix. Traveling to countless airfields and embarkation points on both coasts, they headed for duty stations around the globe.

Some left home to work in the great American defense plants that poured out a torrent of ships, planes, jeeps, tanks, shoes, and guns to supply and move the vast armies of America and her allies.

My mom traveled, too. Like millions of other American women, she traveled into men's territory. Big Mama became 'Rosie the Riveter,' welding the steel of America at a time when America produced more ships and armament than any nation in the history of the planet. We have snapshots of my parents at Virginia Beach for their combination wedding/honeymoon/pre-embarkation stay.

In that smaller world, our parents made friends with people they were unlikely to have met under ordinary circumstances. Dave Powers, a Kennedy family friend and one of my father's buddies in China, said that someday young Joe Kennedy would be President of the United States. My father scoffed at the idea that any son of old Joe, the Ambassador, could ever overcome the father's bad name and win the Presidency. After JFK's election, my father received a letter from Dave Powers on White House stationary inviting him to Washington to see the impossible for himself.

Like millions of American kids, I sat by my father's side in front of the television and watched stories of World War II on programs like *The Twentieth Century* and *Victory at Sea*. We, the babies born after the war, were drawn into the corners of that smaller world. Through television, I saw my father's India and China, the great Pacific Island battles of my uncle, and the Europe of my neighbors.

We watched film clips of our neighbors at Normandy, beginning the 'beginning of the end.' We watched as they and their comrades threw themselves against the withering fire of Normandy's defenses to take the first steps onto the European continent for the final push for the end. 'Nuts' and 'I shall return' had specific meaning for us. We knew the insignias of the 101st and the 82nd and, for me, the special India-China-Burma patch. Like no other event, World War II was the defining expression of American unity in the 20th century.

The generation that landed on the Normandy beaches 50 years ago this week, and the nation that supported that landing, stood unified in the conviction that they were acting for the betterment of the world and the advancement of mankind. I believe their notion of a noble American motive bears the test of time.

In the fifty years since D-Day, we've watched the world expand and fragment, first into centers of competing ideology and then into tribalism. As for the Normandy survivors and their contemporaries, now aged in their seventies and eighties, their selfless courage and sacrifice fifty years ago may have provided the most magnificent example of a generation's altruistic idealism in American history, perhaps in the history of the world.

Gordian resolutions–not

(1993)

I've been thinking about New Year's resolutions. Well, more particularly, I've been rethinking my New Year's resolution. Like most people's, mine is really an old, unresolved problem. I know folks who've determined to diet, quit cigarettes, give the smelly dog a bath. Fortunately, I don't have a dog, don't smoke, and wouldn't dream of messing with my chow or snacks.

My resolution falls directly into the Gordian Knot category. If the Knot were not already named after Gordius, my resolution would be what Gordian-Knot-type problems are called. Folks would say, "This is as tough as sorting through Ilan's Slides."

Believe me, if old Gordo saw my closet jammed-packed with cardboard boxes filled with 20,000 loose slides, he'd thank his lucky stars for the little kink in his rope.

Sorting the slides is such a gargantuan undertaking that I cheated the new year. Last week, I opened the closet door, dragged out a cardboard box, and started to sort.

But no one really has 20,000 slides dumped into boxes, you say.

Don't bet the farm on it. Whenever I needed space in a slide carousel, I'd just dump the slides out of any full one I could lay my hands on. Some folks are destined to make up for a lifetime of dump-outs with sort-outs down the line. That's me. But, I digress.

For two-and-a-half-bucks, I bought a little hand-held viewer and started to write information on each slide. I marked the year the slide was taken, the subject of the picture, and put a little 'x' on the bottom because slides have to go into the projector bottoms-up.

I was on my third slide when I came across a picture of Tamara wearing a pink dance-recital costume with white fringe. The pink color clashed with her flaming-red hair that had been braided into a pigtail and tied back for the recital. Tamara smiled for the camera, her front teeth missing. I called for Jody to come and see how our little girl looked 21 years ago on recital day.

Jody took the loupe from my hand and moved the eyepiece around to find a good light source. Squinting down the tube, she broke into a wide grin. Her teeth flashed in the light. My heart leapt. I wished I had my camera ready to catch that smile on film.

Jody dropped the slide into the box, then reached in, picked up another, and slid it into the loupe. She laughed "Oh look, it's my little Zevi driving his bulldozer. Oh, my beautiful boy."

She flipped the slide back into the box and took out another, and another, and another, without so much as marking even a single one with an 'x.'

I wrestled the loupe away from her and banished her from the den.

I slipped another slide into the loupe and held it to the light. There was Jody. Waist-length, ironed-straight, dark hair, Jody. Bell-bottom jeans, Jody. Hand-sewn, white blouse cross-stitched with blue embroidery, Jody. All 92 pounds of five-foot-two, Jody. In the picture, she pushed a stroller in Harvard Square. In the stroller, our two-year-old, Tamara. Jody mugged for the camera, her dark eyes laughing, white teeth flashing.

I looked at Jody's smile and I had to laugh back. She was smiling for me across the years. Laughing for me as if she knew that, somewhere in time, I'd look at this picture and experience the same tug at my heart that touched me back in Cambridge the moment I snapped it. It was an instant of pure joy with one of those laughs of hers that would last for our whole lives. I held the slide to the light and stared at it for a long time.

Only 19,996 more slides to sort through, Gordius. At this rate, I'll be mythology myself before I finish. What the heck, maybe this year I'll look—next year, I'll sort.

Reflections on a New Year's Eve
(1993)

It was on New Year's Eve that I visited my father for the last time. Jody and I were on our way to toast the waning minutes of 1983 with old friends, but first we would stop at my father's hospital room to spend time with him before the year turned. We didn't know this would be our last visit.

I have forgotten many of the details. I don't remember what his room looked like and I'm surprised that I barely remember what my father looked like that night. Those images are gone from my memory.

But what has stayed with me is the image of my father's eyes. They are what I see when I think of him that New Year's Eve. I remember how his eyes held mine and how, sometime during that visit, my father and I understood that we had been granted this time to speak, to share an intimacy that only the luckiest people, perhaps once in an entire lifetime of words, ever experience.

Ours was a quiet conversation. Not the quiet of illness or infirmity. Not the quiet of sadness or remorse. But the quiet of simple fulfillment. We visited as old friends, aware that now was our last time together, father and son, parent and child, friend and friend.

Even as he had passed his genes on to me, he had given me a system of values and a way of understanding the world. Yet, with all we had in common, my father and I were very different. We each reflected the origins and circumstances of our separate worlds and these were reflected in how we lived our lives. He was born on a far away continent in a hungry village erased from the map long ago. I was a child of America's prosperity living a life he'd dreamed for me. His eyes were blue, mine brown, but down behind the pigment, we mirrored each other's soul.

Eyes don't age. His were as translucent as a clear summer sky, as transparent as pure water. Even as a young boy, I was aware of an age-less mischief alive in my father's eyes. A kid lived there. A kid a lot like me. A sprite who watched my adventures with kindred delight, but who could be hurt like any child can be. At times I caused him hurt. But even then, his eyes said he understood me and even encouraged the struggle between us, the struggle bonding us forever through our own free choice.

On that New Year's Eve 1983, frozen capillaries had stolen much of the use from my father's legs and had chilled his hands. His heart had been racked and starved of blood, deprived by arteries constricted at their shores. But somehow, he'd willed heat into each heart beat. He'd kept that pump going, through each painful beat.

I was there that New Year's Eve. My father needed to be with me then and I with him. Each of us could have predicted what we'd say, things said before, and some things that should have been said but never were, until then. Being together that night, speaking the words, laughing at the old tales and looking into each other's faces, we rein-forced the bonds of a lifetime. They would have to sustain us through the coming absence.

New Year's Eve is a time of meeting and parting and we parted as old friends.

In the waning embers of the year, his blue eyes and my brown held each other for the last time. We nodded our understanding that, between us, it had always been this quiet love even when it had also been sparks and fire. I was proud this man was my father. He was proud I was his son.

We parted with an embrace so close that it was as if our common genetic code reached for its history and entrusted its future. There were no struggles left between us. Only our love was left for this private time.

We had different destinations to pursue that night. I walked into the hospital lobby and found that I needed to rest. I sat in the darkened room and my body shook at what had transpired between us. A time to say good-bye had been a gift. I'd always known the truth of what had passed between us that night but it was a gift to be able to hear it and speak it. In that lobby, I asked the God of Gifts to keep good watch over my father.

That night, my father willed sleep to still the furnace that had warmed his body throughout life. I would see him once again but when next I looked into those eyes, they were no longer his. He was gone.

Tonight, as the minutes before year's-end approach, my thoughts turn back to that New Year's Eve and I see myself reflected once again in my father's clear blue eyes.

About the author

Ilan Fisher: Writer/Photographer:

Ilan Fisher lives in Sharon, Massachusetts with his wife, Jody, and son, Zev. His daughter, Tamara, is an attorney in Boston.

He won nine New England Press Association (NEPA) and Massachusetts Press Association (MPA) awards, including three first-place awards, between 1993-1997. He was recognized by NEPA for both his serious and humorous columns in the same year.

His work has appeared in *The Sharon Advocate* and many other Community Newspaper Company (CNC) newspapers. Additional publications include: *The Foxboro Reporter, WBUR radio, The Mountain Villager,* and *Cranberries Magazine* (for photography, including the cover).

Acknowlegments

The author would like to thank: Jonathan Draudt, Tom Glynn, Joanne Douglas, Tom Quin, Mark and Pat Olken, Jack Authelet, Melody Howard Ritt, Fred Lewis, Mark Jurkowitz, and Dan Rosenfeld for all their help and support during the publication of this volume.